THE BATTLE
Belongs to the
LORD

THE BATTLE
Belongs to the
LORD

Overcoming Life's Struggles
through Worship

~

JOYCE MEYER

New York   Boston   Nashville

FaithWords Edition
Copyright © 2002 by Joyce Meyer
Life In The Word, Inc.
P.O. Box 655
Fenton, Missouri 63026

FaithWords
Hachette Book Group
237 Park Avenue
New York, NY 10017
Visit our Web site at www.faithwords.com

Printed in the United States of America

First Special Sales Edition: February 2003
10 9 8 7

FaithWords is a division of Hachette Book Group, Inc.
The FaithWords name and logo are trademarks of Hachette Book Group, Inc.

ISBN 978-0-446-69213-7

Contents

PART 1: *The Battle Belongs to the Lord*

1   Phase 1 — Hear Directly from God   3

2   Phase 2 — Admit Your Dependence on God   15

3   Phase 3 — Take Your Position   23

4   Phase 4 — The Lord Brings the Deliverance   39

PART 2: *Transformed through Worship*

5   Elijah Stayed in Position   55

6   Don't Wrestle — Worship   61

7   Be Transfigured   77

8   Worship and Prayer   87

9   Worship and Change   105

10   Worship God with a Pure Conscience   113

11   Transformation and Transfiguration   123

12   Continue to Behold and Worship   137

13   God Is for Us!   143

14   God Will Provide   149

15   God Is on My Side!   157

16   Remain in Position   169

17   For the Lord Was with Him   177

18   The Devil Means Evil, but God Means Good   181

Conclusion   195

Prayer for a Personal Relationship with the Lord   199

Endnotes   203

Part
1

The Battle Belongs to the Lord

Chapter

1

Phase 1 —
Hear Directly from God

G od wants us to be totally free from fear. He doesn't want us to live in torment, and He doesn't want fear to stop us from confidently doing what He tells us to do. When we have a deep understanding concerning God's perfect unconditional love for us, we realize He will always take care of everything that concerns us — that knowledge eventually delivers us from fear. As we have experience with God and see that He always takes care of us and provides what we need, we begin to relax.

> *There is no fear in love [dread does not exist], but full-grown (complete, perfect) love turns fear out of doors and expels every trace of terror! For fear brings with it the thought of punishment, and [so] he who is afraid has not reached the full maturity of love [is not yet grown into love's complete perfection].*

> 1 John 4:18

God moves on our behalf when we focus on Him instead of on our fears. The feeling of fear or fearful thoughts is simply our enemy Satan trying to distract us from God and His will for our lives. We may feel fear at various times in our lives but we can choose to trust God and if we need to, "do it afraid."

This "do it afraid" theory is something God revealed to me many years ago. I saw that when He told Joshua as recorded

3

in Joshua 1 to "fear not," He was actually warning him that fear would try to stop him, but instead of letting the fear control him, he was encouraged to be strong and full of courage and keep going forward.

> *For God has not given us a spirit of fear, but of power and of love and of a sound mind.*
>
> 2 TIMOTHY 1:7 NKJV

Anytime trouble comes fear is usually the first thing we feel. Satan injects "what if" thoughts into our head, and we often begin to see the worst possible outcome. As soon as that happens, we should realize what is going on — Satan is trying to keep us from going forward in God's will and good plan for our lives.

When we feel fear or begin to experience fearful thoughts, the very first thing we should do is pray. I always say, "Pray about everything and fear nothing." We should set ourselves to seek God until we know we have the emotional and mental victory over the spirit of fear. As we seek God, we are focusing on Him instead of on our fears. We worship Him for Who He is and express our appreciation to Him for the good He has done, is doing and will continue to do.

God has blessings and new opportunities in store for us. To receive them we must take steps of faith. That often means doing things we don't feel like doing or in our own minds don't even think will work, but our trust and reverence for God must be greater than what we personally want, think or feel.

We see a perfect example of this in Luke Chapter 5. Peter and some of the other disciples of Jesus had been fishing all night; they had caught nothing; they were tired, actually exhausted; they needed sleep; I am sure they were hungry. They had just finished washing and storing their nets, which was a big job. Jesus appeared on the bank of the lake and told them if they wanted to catch a haul of fish, they should cast their nets again, only this time in deeper water. Peter explained to the Lord that they were exhausted; they had caught nothing, but he said, "On the ground of Your word we will lower the nets again." This is the kind of attitude the Lord wants us to have. We may not feel like doing something; we may not want to; we may not think it is a good idea; we may feel fearful that none of it will work, but we should be willing to obey God rather than our fears or feelings.

The devil tries to use fear in its many different forms to keep us in shallow water. But even though we may feel fear, we need to focus our attention on God, and at His word we should launch out into the deep to receive the blessings God has for us.

After this, the Moabites, the Ammonites, and with them the Meunites came against Jehoshaphat to battle.

2 CHRONICLES 20:1

Are the "-ites" after you? In this passage it was the Moabites, the Ammonites and the Menuites who were after King Jehosaphat and the people of Judah. In other places in the Old Testament it was the Jebusites, the Hittites and the Canaanites who were the troublemakers for God's people.

But with us it is the "fear-ites," the "disease-ites," "poverty-ites," "bad marriage-ites," "stress-ites," "grouchy neighbor-ites," "insecurity-ites," "rejection-ites" and on and on.

How many "-ites" are chasing you around? However many there are, let's look at what King Jehoshaphat did to turn His attention on God instead of focusing on all those "-ites" that were trying to rise and rule.

SEEK "A WORD" FROM THE LORD

It was told Jehoshaphat, A great multitude has come against you from beyond the [Dead] Sea, from Edom; and behold they are in Hazazon-tamar, which is En-gedi.

Then Jehoshaphat feared, and set himself [determinedly, as his vital need] to seek the Lord; he proclaimed a fast in all Judah.

2 CHRONICLES 20:2,3

When Jehoshaphat was told that the "-ites" were coming against him, the first thing he did was fear. But then he did something else: He set himself to seek the Lord. Determined to hear from Him, he even proclaimed a fast throughout the land for that very purpose. He knew he needed to hear from God. He needed a battle plan, and only God could give him one that was sure to succeed.

We should develop the habit of running to God when we have trouble instead of to people. We should seek God rather than our own minds or other people's minds. Ask yourself, "When trouble comes, do I run to the phone or the throne?" God might direct us to a person for advice, but we should always go to Him first to show that we honor and trust Him.

Phase 1 of God's battle plan is to combat fear by hearing from God. Romans 10:17 teaches us that **faith comes by hearing, and hearing by the word of God** (NKJV). This verse is not referring to the written Word of God, but the spoken Word of God. It is called *rhema* in the original language of the New Testament, which is Greek. In other words when we hear from God, faith fills our hearts and drives the fear away. Jehoshaphat knew he had to hear from God, and we have the same need.

God may speak by giving us peace deep inside of us; He may give a creative idea; He may calm our troubled emotions; He may give us assurance. God speaks in various ways, but if we seek Him we will find Him. He will lead us and guide us if we acknowledge Him in all our ways. (Proverbs 3:5,6.)

Everyone you know may be telling you to trust God, and you want to, but "how to" has evaded you. The fears are screaming at you, threatening you. Your friends are saying, "Everything will be all right," but somehow it doesn't penetrate the fear until God speaks deep in your heart and says, "You can trust Me; I will take care of this; everything is going to be all right."

In 1989 I went to the doctor for a regular checkup. He discovered a small lump in my breast and wanted me to go immediately for a biopsy. I went thinking it would be nothing, but the outcome was that I had a very fast growing type of cancer, and surgery was highly recommended immediately.

I can remember walking down the hall in my house, and fear hitting me so strongly that I felt like I was going to fall down. My knees would actually feel as if they were going to buckle under me. Every night when I went to bed, I had a hard time going to sleep. Even when I did sleep, it was not a good, solid, restful sleep; it was a fitful sleep. Every so often I would wake up, and there the fears would be pounding at my mind.

"Cancer" is a word that comes with great fear. No matter how many of my family members or friends told me God would take care of it, I was still battling fear until one of those nights about three o'clock in the morning when God spoke deep inside of my heart and said, "Joyce, you can trust Me." After that, I did not experience the sickening fear again. I was apprehensive as I waited for the results from my lymph nodes test to see if I would need further treatment, but I still knew that I was in God's hands and whatever happened, He would take care of me.

As it turned out, I did not need any further treatment. We actually realized that through early detection, God had saved my life. I ended up thankful instead of fearful, and Satan lost another battle.

JEHOSHAPHAT NEEDED TO HEAR FROM GOD

When Jehoshaphat heard that a huge army was amassing to attack Judah, he knew what to do. He needed to set himself to seek — not the advice of people — his friends, family or advisors — but to hear from God.

Jehoshaphat had probably been involved in other battles previously — why couldn't he just use some of the same methods he used before? No matter how many times something has worked in the past, it may not work to solve the current crisis unless God anoints it afresh. He may anoint an old method, but He may also give us fresh direction we have never had before. We must look to God not to methods. He does use methods, but they have no power unless He is working through them. We cannot focus on methods anymore than we can on fears. Our focus, our source of supply, must be God and Him alone. Our answer is not in methods but in relationship with God.

Woe to those who go down to Egypt for help, who rely on horses and trust in chariots because they are many and in horsemen because they are very strong, but they look not to the Holy One of Israel, nor seek and consult the Lord!

ISAIAH 31:1

I have never discovered exactly what "woe" is, but I know I don't want any of it. Woe is obviously a sorrowful thing; it is trouble and misery. When we seek God we have peace and joy, so why would we choose woe resulting from seeking the world?

JEHOSHAPHAT'S VITAL NEED

Jehoshaphat knew that unless he heard from God, he was not going to make it. That need was what *The Amplified Bible* calls his "vital need." There are some things we can do without, but others are vital. Jehoshaphat knew having God's direction was vital.

You may be in a similar situation to Jehoshaphat's. You too may need a word from God. You may feel that, like a drowning man or woman, you are going under for the third time. You may desperately need a personal word from the Lord if you are to survive.

God wants to speak to you even more than you want to hear from Him. Seek Him by giving Him your time, and you will not be disappointed.

Jehoshaphat proclaimed a fast in all Judah, and Judah gathered to seek the Lord for help, yearning for Him with all their desire.

And Judah gathered together to ask help from the Lord; even out of all the cities of Judah they came to seek the Lord [yearning for Him with all their desire].

And Jehoshaphat stood in the assembly of Judah and Jerusalem in the house of the Lord before the new court

And said, O Lord, God of our fathers, are You not God in heaven? And do You not rule over all the kingdoms of the nations? In Your hand are power and might, so that none is able to withstand You.

2 CHRONICLES 20:4-6

Jehoshaphat proclaimed a fast to show his sincerity to God. Missing a few meals and taking that time to seek God is not a bad idea. Turning the television off and spending the time you would normally spend watching it with God is not a bad idea either. Stay home a few evenings and spend extra time with the Lord instead of going out with your friends and repeating your problem over and over to them. These things and others show that we know hearing from God is vital. I have learned the word *seek* means to pursue, crave, and go after with all your might. In other words we act like a starving man in search of food to keep us alive.

I would also like to add that we need to seek God all the time not just when we are in trouble. Once God spoke to me that the reason so many people had problems all the time was because that was the only time they would seek Him. He showed me that if He removed the problems, He would not get any time with the people. He said, "Seek Me as if you were desperate all the time and then you won't find yourself desperate as often in reality." I think this is good advice, and I highly recommend that we all follow it.

TALK TO GOD ABOUT HIM

Instead of immediately presenting the problem to the Lord, Jehoshaphat began to talk to the Lord about how mighty the Lord is. He turned his focus on the Lord instead of on his fear of the problem.

> *And said, O Lord, God of our fathers, are You not God in heaven? And do You not rule over all the kingdoms of the nations? In Your hand are power and might, so that none is able to withstand You.*
>
> 2 CHRONICLES 20:6

Instead of talking to God only about our problems, we need to talk to Him about Him. We need to talk to Him about Who He is, about the power of His Name and the power of the blood of His Son Jesus, about the great things we know that He can perform and has already performed. After we have praised and worshiped Him in this way, then we can begin to mention the problem. I would not like it if my children only came to talk to me when they had problems — I want them to fellowship with me.

I can think of a few people right now who only call me when they have problems, and it hurts me. I feel that they don't really care about me, but only what they want me to do for them. I am sure you have experienced this and feel the same way. These people may call themselves friends, but in reality they are not. Friends are for times of trouble, but that is not all they are for. As a friend, we need to show appreciation and spend time encouraging those we are in relationship with. We must avoid being the type of people who are what I call "takers." Those who always take but never give.

I want to be the friend of God. He called Abraham His friend, and I want that also. The Lord is not just my problem solver, He is my everything, and I appreciate Him more than I know how to say.

"Now, Lord, Behold Our Problem"

Did not You, O our God, drive out the inhabitants of this land before Your people Israel and give it forever to the descendants of Abraham Your friend?

They dwelt in it and have built You a sanctuary in it for Your Name, saying,

If evil comes upon us, the sword of judgment, or pestilence, or famine, we will stand before this house and before You — for Your Name [and the symbol of Your presence] is in this house — and cry to You in our affliction, and You will hear and save.

And now behold, the men of Ammon, Moab, and Mount Seir, whom You would not let Israel invade when they came from the land of Egypt, and whom they turned from and did not destroy —

Behold, they reward us by coming to drive us out of Your possession which You have given us to inherit.

2 Chronicles 20:7-11

These are fighting words. If we will listen to what the Lord is saying to us through them, we will learn something that will change our battle plan forever and give us victory after victory.

After starting his prayer by acknowledging how great, awesome, powerful and wonderful the Lord is, Jehoshaphat then began relating specific mighty acts the Lord had performed in the past to protect His people and uphold the promises He had made them. And in finally presenting his request, He began by expressing His confidence that the Lord would handle the problem. Jehoshaphat said in so many words, "Oh, by the way, our enemies are coming against us to try to take away the possession that you gave us for our inheritance. I just thought I would mention this little problem. But You are so great; I know You already have it all under control."

When we do ask God for help we should realize He hears us the first time we ask Him for something. We don't need to spend our prayer time asking Him for the same thing over and over. We may keep talking to Him about our needs until we have assurance in our hearts that we have a breakthrough, but we don't have to do that to move God.

God has a plan for our deliverance before the problem ever appears. God is not surprised when the enemy attacks. He is not in heaven wringing His hands trying to figure out what to do. Our part is to focus on Him and His mighty power, worshiping Him and praising Him for the manifestation of His solution and listening for a word or direction from Him.

Chapter
2

Phase 2 —
Admit Your Dependence on God

<hr>

O our God, will You not exercise judgment upon them? For we have no might to stand against this great company that is coming against us. We do not know what to do, but our eyes are upon You.

2 CHRONICLES 20:12

Now we come into phase two of God's battle plan for Jehoshaphat, which is found in verse 12. Here Jehoshaphat admits to God openly his total inability to deal with the problem.

We need to realize that we cannot solve the problems that face us in life. We don't have the answers to every question. We don't know how to deal with every situation we encounter. Like Jehoshaphat, we just don't know what to do.

Instead of spinning our wheels, trying to do something about something we can't do anything about until we are completely exhausted and totally frustrated from struggling, we need to let God do for us what we cannot do for ourselves.

For years I tried very hard to change myself without success. I tried so hard and so long to break bad habits only to fail time and time again. I tried to alter different things in my life, to get prosperity, to make my ministry grow and to be healed. I was constantly battling with all the "-ites." I remember wanting to give up simply because I was so exhausted from trying to fight my own battles.

I went through all that on a regular basis until one day I was being really kind of melodramatic about it, trying to impress God with how miserable I was. I said something like, "God, I've had it. This is it. I'm through. Nothing I'm doing is working. I give up. I'm not going to do this anymore."

Just then, deep inside me, I heard the Holy Spirit say, "Really?" There was real excitement in His voice. That happens because the only time He gets to work in us is when we become so exhausted that we finally decide, "Instead of trying to do this myself, I'm going to give up and let God be God."

Trying to be God will wear you out fast. Why not give up your own effort and do what Jehoshaphat did in verse 12? Admit to God that you have no might to stand against your enemies and that you don't know what to do, but you are looking to Him for direction and deliverance.

THREE IMPORTANT THINGS TO DO

The three things Jehoshaphat did were very important. 1) He admitted that he had no might to stand against his enemies; 2) he admitted that he did not know what to do; 3) he said that his eyes were on God.

By saying those three things, Jehoshaphat got himself in position for a miracle, and it did not seem to take him very long either. It only took him twelve verses. Most of us can't get there in twelve years, let alone in twelve verses.

A Position of Total Dependence on God

Jesus said, . . . **apart from me you can do nothing** (John 15:5 NIV). The first time I read that Scripture I did not even begin to realize how true it was. I was a very independent person, and God began speaking this Scripture to me early in my walk with Him. One of the spiritual laws of receiving from God is entire dependence upon Him. Without faith we cannot please God. It is the channel through which we receive from Him. Faith is described in *The Amplified Bible* as the leaning of the entire human personality in absolute trust in His power, wisdom and goodness. (See 2 Timothy 1:5.)

We are to lean on, rely only and entirely depend on Him, taking all the weight off of ourselves and putting it all on Him. When I plop down in a big easy chair, I am putting my entire dependence on that chair to hold me. I take all the weight off myself and put all of it on the chair. It is amazing that we trust a chair more than we do God many times.

We say we lean on God, and perhaps we do partially, but we have difficulty leaning entirely on Him. We often have a backup plan just in case God does not come through.

Let's do a recap. When the "-ites" came against Jehoshaphat, what did he do to get direction on how to fight his battle? The first thing he did was set himself to seek God: "Whatever it takes, I am going to seek God. This situation is so serious that I am even going to fast because I know I need to hear from God."

Then he began to talk to God about His character. Finally, he mentioned the problem but only after praise and worship. Next, he openly admitted his entire dependence on God. He said what we often have a hard time saying: "I don't know what to do."

To many of us, saying, "I don't know what to do," is embarrassing. We feel that it is our duty to figure things out. We feel stupid or insufficient if we cannot come up with answers. That is the reason why we often keep trying different things, even though none of them is working. Man has an inherent desire in his flesh to receive credit and be well thought of, but God says His glory belongs to Him. Although He does glorify us, it is HIS glory He gives us and not something we have earned.

I believe that the devil assigns demons every morning to sit on each of our shoulders and whisper in our ears, "What are you going to do? What are you going to do? What are you going to do?"

Jehoshaphat didn't feel stupid, and neither should we. He told God, "We don't know what to do, and even if we did, we wouldn't have the strength to do it." By saying this and meaning it, he put himself in a position of total dependence upon God. He did it early in the battle — the sooner we depend entirely on God, the sooner we will have the victory.

Without God's help, we can't change anything in our lives. We can't change ourselves, our spouse, our family, our friends or our circumstances. Truly, truly, apart from Him we cannot do anything!

We forfeit peace and joy due to not letting God be God. We try to figure out things we have no business even touching with our minds. There are some things that are simply too high or too deep for us. Nothing is too hard or too wonderful for God, but many things are too hard or too wonderful for us. God is infinite, but we are finite human beings with limitations. God has surpassing knowledge, but ours is limited. First Corinthians 13:9 says that our knowledge is fragmentary, or partial. We know some things, but we don't know everything. There are some things we just need to leave alone. We won't know everything, but we can grow to a place where we are satisfied to know the One Who knows. When we arrive at that place, we enter God's rest, which also releases joy in our lives. In Psalm 131:1 David wrote: LORD, **my heart is not haughty, nor my eyes lofty; neither do I exercise myself in matters too great or in things too wonderful for me.** That is the attitude of heart God wants all of us to have.

It is so liberating to say, "Lord, I don't know what to do, and even if I did, I couldn't do it. But, Lord, my eyes are on You. I am going to wait and watch for You to do something about this situation — because there is absolutely nothing I can do about it."

When we are faced with impossible or even difficult situations, we may hear that recording playing in our heads, "What are you going to do? What are you going to do? What are you going to do?" Our friends may say, "I heard about your situation. What are you going to do?"

That is when we should tell them, "I'm going to do what Jehoshaphat did in 2 Chronicles 20. I'm going to turn it over to the Lord — and wait on Him. He will do something wonderful, and I am going to enjoy watching Him do it!

WAIT ON THE LORD

And all Judah stood before the Lord, with their children and their wives.

2 CHRONICLES 20:13

I really love this verse. I recognize it as a power verse. Standing still is action in God's economy. It is spiritual action. We usually take action in the natural and spiritually we do nothing, but in waiting on God and standing before the Lord, Jehoshaphat took spiritual action. He was saying in effect, "Lord, I am going to wait on You until You do something about this situation. In the meantime, I am going to enjoy my life while I am waiting for You to move."

Satan hates our joy. It is the opposite of what he is trying to provoke. He wants to see anger, unbridled emotion, tears, self-pity, grumbling, complaining, blaming God and others for our situation. He wants to see anything but joy; *Nehemiah 8:10 says that the joy of the Lord is our strength.*

It is not irresponsible to enjoy life while we are waiting on God to solve our problems. Jesus said, **The thief comes only in order to steal and kill and destroy. I came that they [you] may have and enjoy life, and have it in abundance (to the full, till it overflows) (John 10:10).**

We are tempted to think that we are not doing our part if we don't worry or try to figure out some answer, but we must resist that temptation because it prevents our deliverance rather than aiding in it.

Faced with an overwhelming force that was descending upon them to enslave them and destroy their land, all of Judah came and stood there before the Lord.

All the time the devil was screaming at them, "What are you going to do? What are you going to do? What are you going to do?"

But they just stood there, waiting on God.

In Isaiah 40:31 (KJV), we read, . . . **they that wait upon the LORD shall renew their strength; they shall mount up with wings as eagles; they shall run, and not be weary; and they shall walk, and not faint.**

We may need the strength we gain while waiting in order to do whatever it is God will instruct us to do when He gives us direction. Those who wait on the Lord are the ones who receive answers and the ones who are strong enough to follow God's direction once they receive it.

WAITING FOR THE ANSWER

Then the Spirit of the Lord came upon Jahaziel son of Zechariah, the son of Benaiah, the son of Jeiel, the son of Mattaniah, a Levite of the sons of Asaph, in the midst of the assembly.

He said, Hearken, all Judah, you inhabitants of Jerusalem, and you King Jehoshaphat. The Lord says this to you: Be not afraid or dismayed at this great multitude; for the battle is not yours, but God's.

2 CHRONICLES 20:14,15

When all of Judah was assembled before the Lord, one of their number began to prophesy. The Spirit of God came on him because they were all waiting on God.

When we learn to seek God and wait on Him, He will give us an answer. That answer may be very plain and simple. The Lord told Judah to not be afraid because the battle was not to be their battle, but the Lord's. That does not sound too mystical or deeply spiritual, but it was all they needed to hear.

What good news that must have been to Jehoshaphat and the rest of the people. THE BATTLE IS NOT YOURS, BUT GOD'S. That did not mean there was nothing for them to do; it meant that God was going to show them their part. They could do it in the strength and wisdom of the Lord, but the battle was still His to win.

After that word of encouragement came a word of instruction, as we will see. We are to wait on the Lord until He has told us what we are to do — and then do it in His strength that we have gained while waiting on Him.

Chapter
3

Phase 3 — Take Your Position

===

Tomorrow go down to them. Behold, they will come up the Ascent of Ziz, and you will find them at the end of the ravine before the wilderness of Jeruel.

You shall not need to fight in this battle; take your positions, stand still, and see the deliverance of the Lord [Who is] with you, O Judah and Jerusalem. Fear not nor be dismayed. . . .

2 CHRONICLES 20:16,17

This passage instructs the people of Judah in the position they were to take for the battle. I always thought their position and ours was to stand still. Although that is true, there was another instruction that was equally important. After receiving this instruction from the Lord, Jehoshaphat bowed on his knees with his face to the ground and worshiped. WOW! Worship was their actual position, and in worshiping they would also be standing still. On our knees is a battle position — the reverent position of face bowed to the ground is a battle position. Kneeling with uplifted hands is a battle position. David said of God, "He teaches my hands to war." I believe that he was taught to lift up his hands in worship and surrender to the Lord, and He recognized it as a battle position.

Blessed be the Lord, my Rock and my keen and firm Strength, Who teaches my hands to war and my fingers to fight —

PSALM 144:1

Perhaps when David played his musical instruments, his fingers were fighting. Praise, worship, singing, God's Word, joy — all of these are weapons of warfare.

A primary definition of *praise* in Vine's dictionary of Old Testament words lists the terms "glory; praise; song of praise; praiseworthy deeds."[1] In the New Testament *praise* is defined in Vine's dictionary of Greek words in part as "primarily 'a tale, narration.'"[2] It continues to say that "'praise' is to be ascribed to God, in respect of His glory (the exhibition of His character and operations). . . ."[3] In other words, to praise means to talk about or sing out about the goodness, grace and greatness of God.

In the Old Testament *to worship* is described as "prostrate oneself, bow down."[4] In the New Testament *worship* is defined in part as, "to make obeisance, do reverence to" from a word formed by two Greek words meaning "towards," and "to kiss" "used of an act of homage or reverence" to God.[5] Listed under "Notes" a reference in Acts 17:25 to the word meaning "to serve, do service to" God "is rendered 'is worshiped'" in some translations.[6] Also under "Notes" Vine's says this: "(1) The worship of God is nowhere defined in Scripture. A consideration of the above verbs shows that it is not confined to praise; broadly it may be regarded as the direct acknowledgement to God, of His nature, attributes, ways and claims, whether by the outgoing of the heart in praise and thanksgiving or by deed done in such acknowledgment. . . ."[7]

These are basic and simple definitions, but I feel it is all we need. If God didn't bother to define worship in the Bible, He obviously knew that people have an inherent understanding of what it is.

For the weapons of our warfare are not physical [weapons of flesh and blood], but they are mighty before God for the overthrow and destruction of strongholds.

2 CORINTHIANS 10:4

Our weapons are not natural weapons. They are not something the world would understand, or even anything that would seem in the natural realm to work. But in God's kingdom, they do work. When the Israelites were in battle, they often sent Judah first. Judah was the tribe that represented praise; that is what Judah means. We must learn to fight God's way, not the world's way. **We wrestle [war] not against flesh and blood, but against principalities, against powers, against the rulers of the darkness of this world, against spiritual wickedness in high places** (Ephesians 6:12 KJV).

Our war is not with people of flesh and blood; it is with Satan, the enemy of our souls. Therefore, we take a battle position in the spiritual realm of standing our ground and worshiping the Lord.

Therefore put on God's complete armor, that you may be able to resist and stand your ground on the evil day [of danger], and, having done all [the crisis demands], to stand [firmly in your place].

Stand therefore [hold your ground]. . . .

EPHESIANS 6:13,14

I was so absolutely amazed when I realized that our position in battle was one of worship. I don't know why I didn't see it before unless, of course, Satan clouded my understanding by keeping me busy in works of the flesh, which are works that don't work!

To stand means to abide or to enter God's rest. It is not resting physically, but spiritually. When I am standing my ground, I am refusing to give in. I am persisting in believing that God will deliver me. I am abiding (remaining and continuing) in Him.

Ephesians 6 also tells us to stand our ground: . . . **and having done all, to stand** (verse 13 KJV).

In our battle against our spiritual enemies, our position is in Christ. It is abiding and resting in Him. It is worship and praise.

When you are faced with a crisis and don't know what to do, follow the instructions God gave Jehoshaphat and his people. Take your position (worship); stand still and see the salvation of the Lord. Collect yourself. Calm down. Tell your mind to stop trying to figure out the answer. Turn your focus on God.

Open your mouth, and sing the songs that are in your heart. God says in His Word that He will give us songs of deliverance. God gives them, but we must sing them in order for them to be effective against Satan.

> You are a hiding place for me; You, Lord, preserve me from trouble, You surround me with songs and shouts of deliverance. Selah [Pause, and calmly think of that]!
>
> PSALM 32:7

The Lord told Jehoshaphat not to be dismayed. Dismay is a mixture of fear, worry, panic and anxiety. When one of these "fear-ites" tries to get our attention, we need to **go out against** those kinds of thoughts and feelings.

> . . . *Tomorrow go out against them, for the Lord is with you.*
>
> 2 CHRONICLES 20:17

We need to stand still, and **go out against** those fears by worshiping God. Worshiping God is not only for when we come together in a church service; it is for our everyday lives — private worship. It is something that we all need to do all throughout the day.

The Bible describes a physical posture of worship. After God spoke to Jehoshaphat and the people of Judah through the prophet, the people reacted by bowing down in worship. We cannot always bow down; we may be places where that would not be possible or even appropriate. But in our hearts, we can always worship anytime and in any place.

THE POSTURE OF WORSHIP

> *And Jehoshaphat bowed his head with his face to the ground, and all Judah and the inhabitants of Jerusalem fell down before the Lord, worshiping Him.*
>
> 2 CHRONICLES 20:18

I believe that this verse describes the posture that we need to take before the Lord on a much more regular basis. As I have already said, we may not always be able to take this position, but we should practice actually bowing down before the Lord in reverence and worship. I actually believe that it is good for us as individuals to bow down. It reminds us of our position of humility before the Lord.

I have studied the word "worship" and have discovered that there are several different ways to describe it. Obviously, there is supposed to be an inner heart attitude that comes first, but one of the words that is used frequently to describe worship speaks of an outward posture, as seen in 2 Chronicles 20:18.

STAND UP AND PRAISE GOD

And some Levites of the Kohathites and Korahites stood up to praise the Lord, the God of Israel, with a very loud voice.

2 CHRONICLES 20:19

Get a picture of what happened in this situation. First, everybody bowed down to worship the Lord. Then, some of them stood up and started to praise God **with a very loud voice.**

We don't need to get caught up in position, but we do need to worship on a regular basis. We should worship God because we believe that He deserves our worship, and we should also realize that Satan hates our worship, and it defeats him.

Some people believe that at one time, Satan may have been the archangel in charge of worship in heaven until he rebelled against God and got thrown out and that his body was actually made up of musical instruments, so every movement he made must have created music. No wonder he despises our worship; he is jealous. It was a position he had and lost through rebellion and pride. (See Ezekiel 28:13,14,17.)

BELIEVE AND REMAIN STEADFAST

And they rose early in the morning and went out into the Wilderness of Tekoa; and as they went out, Jehoshaphat stood and said, Hear me, O Judah, and you inhabitants of Jerusalem! Believe in the Lord your God and you shall be established; believe and remain steadfast to His prophets and you shall prosper [or succeed NASB].

2 CHRONICLES 20:20

After they had worshiped and praised the Lord, the people went out to meet the enemy. Please notice that they went out to meet the enemy *after* they had worshiped and praised.

As they went out, Jehoshaphat reminded them that they needed to remember the word of the Lord that had come forth the day before and not start doubting it.

Some of us may need to go back to the word that the Lord gave us. God can speak a comforting word or a word of direction, and we can be very excited, filled with faith, feeling bold and able to conquer the enemy. Yet, we can also forget that word and need to return to it. Timothy had become fearful and discouraged, and Paul encouraged him to remember the words of prophecy that were given him at the time of his ordination and laying on of hands by elders.

Jehoshaphat told the people to believe the prophets, to remember the word the prophet had given the day before that the battle was not theirs but the Lord's. I encourage you not to listen to the enemy. He is a liar and the father of all lies. He is the discourager, the one who whispers, "Your breakthrough will never come." Go to God's written Word or a personal word He has given you at some time, and remember that God cannot lie. His promises are sure, and we can depend on them.

Remain steadfast, and you will be delivered. We inherit the promises of God by faith and patience.

SING PRAISES

When he had consulted with the people, he appointed singers to sing to the Lord and praise Him in their holy [priestly] garments as they went out before the army, saying, Give thanks to the Lord, for His mercy and loving-kindness endure forever!

2 CHRONICLES 20:21

Here in this verse is the essence of this phase of God's battle plan for Jehosaphat and his people: *Sing to the Lord; praise Him and give thanks to Him.* The praisers said, **Give thanks to the Lord, for His mercy and loving-kindness endure forever!**

Singing and giving thanks may not seem like the thing to do in trouble, but believe me, it is exactly what we need to do. Many things don't make sense to our minds, but that does not mean we should not do them. We rely on our minds far too much without realizing many wrong things are programmed into them from years of operating in the world's system. The Bible says in Romans 12:2 that our minds must be entirely renewed by God's Word in order for us to experience His good will for our lives.

Let me give you an example from my own experience and one from a friend of mine.

Years ago I was having some severe headaches, so the doctor put me on some medicine. The medicine made me feel like a freight train was going through my head. I actually had a loud roar in my head that made me feel like I was going crazy.

I had taken the medicine for one day, and that night when I went to bed, I could not sleep. I was sick to my stomach; I had the roar plus the pain in my head, and the devil was busy lying to me. There had been some mental illness in my family bloodline, and Satan was taking advantage of that by telling me that I was losing my mind. Dave was sound asleep; it was about two or three o'clock in the morning; the house was very quiet and I felt all alone in the world with my pain. I felt as if I was going to be sick, so I got up and went to the bathroom.

I was sitting on the bathroom floor with the side of my head and face resting on the toilet seat. Just then I heard a song coming up out of my inner man, and I heard the Holy Spirit say, "Sing."

"Sing?" I thought.

I didn't feel like singing. I felt like throwing up, perhaps giving up — anything but getting up and singing. However, the instruction persisted. "Sing." I felt depressed, like crying, feeling sorry for myself and even getting mad at my husband, Dave, because he was sleeping while I was suffering. We cannot act on our feelings and experience God's victory in our lives.

The song that was rolling around inside me was an old song that I had not heard in many years, a song called "In the Garden."[8] It reminded me of Jesus and how He suffered in the Garden of Gethsemane. Surely if he could make it, so could I. In obedience to God, I opened my mouth and began to croak out the song. I sounded so bad that I can't even say I was singing, but I was trying to obey God, and I did get better.

The second example comes from a friend who was being audited by the IRS, not a very pleasant event to say the least. Although he had done nothing wrong that he knew of, the woman doing the audit was not very friendly and seemed to be looking for something to make trouble about. They had already had two appointments, and he was driving to the third one. He was really trying to reason out what he should say and how he should approach this when suddenly he heard a song come into his heart that he had written. He said the song would not go away, and it began to irritate him because he felt he needed to make his plan, not sing.

This man is a worship leader, so writing and singing songs is very common for him, but he felt the timing was all wrong. He kept resisting the song, even telling the Lord, "This is not the time to be working on a song." God finally got his attention and showed him that this was actually a song of deliverance for him, but he needed to sing it. It was a song about God being our Refuge and Deliverer in times of trouble.

He went on to the appointment, singing all the way. He was filled with joy by the time he arrived and had a very interesting time. He said the IRS agent actually became flustered and confused and could not seem to even understand what she was looking at. He was very cheerful and friendly with her, while she remained sour and somber. She suddenly said, "The appointment is over. I will call to set up another one." Three weeks went by, and he received a letter in the mail saying that everything was fine, and there would be no need for other appointments. The case was closed.

I hope from these two examples that you are encouraged to sing when trouble comes rather than do some of the things you might be tempted to do.

Jehoshaphat probably felt the same way I did on the bathroom floor or my friend did driving to his appointment, but Jehoshaphat was obedient, and it worked, as you will see.

Just Worship

When we have a need in our life, we can worship God for it rather than begging Him for it. The Bible states that we have not because we ask not. (James 4:2.) So we need to ask — we need to make our request known — but we don't need to get into a begging mode. We are believers, not beggars. Matthew 6 teaches us that when we are praying, we are not to repeat the same phrases over and over, thinking that we will be heard for all our speaking. Quality is much more important than quantity. We often have the mistaken idea that if prayers are long, they are effective, but that is not true.

I personally believe that sometimes we can say so much that we are not even sure what we are asking for any longer. I have actually found myself talking so much in prayer that I get confused. A few years ago God was dealing with me about this and challenged me to begin asking Him for what I wanted and needed very simply, using as few words as possible. It took learning a new discipline, but I began to do it. I would then use the rest of my time waiting in His Presence or simply worshiping Him. I found it to be much more refreshing and effective. I often still find myself slipping back into old ways, thinking that more is better, and the Lord has to remind me again that simplicity is powerful.

All we need to do is look at the Lord's Prayer. His disciples said, . . . **Lord, teach us to pray** . . . and the model Jesus gave is extremely simple but certainly gets the job done. It is the sincerity of the heart that is important to the Lord, not a bunch of empty words that possibly have no real heart sincerity behind them.

I am not suggesting that we don't spend a lot of time with the Lord, but that time can be spent waiting and worshiping, as well as talking.

I feel that the best way to see our needs met is to ask for what we want, or need, and then worship God that *He* is what we need. He does not just give us what we need — He is what we need.

When we need peace, He is our peace. He is our sanctification, our justification and our righteousness. He is Jehovah-Jireh, the Lord our Provider. It is the joy of the Lord that is our strength. He does not just give us joy; He is our joy, our hope and the Way.

One of the things that I have noticed happening in my life is that when I worship God for one of His attributes, I see that attribute released into my life. If we need mercy, we should begin to worship and praise God for His mercy. If we need provision or finances, we should begin to worship and praise God that He has already promised us that we will never lack any good thing. (See Psalm 84:11.) We can rejoice in the fact that because He is our Shepherd, we shall not want.

You might try saying something like this:

"Father, I come in Jesus' Name, and I worship You for Your awesome majesty. I know, God, that You can do anything. I remember all the times you have helped and delivered me in the past, and I want to thank You for Your goodness in my life. You, Lord, are my Helper, my Strength, my High Tower, a Refuge in the storm; You are my Hiding Place.

"You are faithful, and I choose to place my faith in You. Father, You know that I have a need right now. My enemies are coming hard against me, and I don't know what to do. Even if I did, I wouldn't be strong enough to do it without You. I am waiting on You, Lord, to give me the victory. The battle belongs to You, Lord; it is not mine.

"Deliver me however You choose. Your will be done, not mine. My times are in Your hands. Now, Lord, I praise and worship You that You have a plan and that no person or demonic power can divert Your plan. I thank You that You are in the process of delivering me right now, and I will see that deliverance with my own eyes. Thank You, Lord, for giving me peace while I wait. Thank You for strength not to give up. Help me to walk in the fruit of the Spirit, even though I am being pressured right now by the enemy. Keep me on the narrow path that leads the way to life. I love You more than I know how to say."

Then as the need comes to mind through the days ahead, just begin to praise, worship and give thanks that God has heard your prayer and is working to give you the victory.

This kind of praying will actually encourage you and increase your faith.

RELEASE THROUGH WORSHIP

There is a release that comes through worship. Sometimes we need a mental or emotional release. As we worship the Lord,

THE BATTLE BELONGS TO THE LORD

we release the emotional or mental burden that is weighing us down. It is swallowed up in the awesomeness of God.

Begin to worship early in the morning. I suggest starting before you even get out of bed. Worship while you get ready for work; worship on the way to work. You will be amazed to see how things begin to change at home and on the job. Worship creates an atmosphere where God can work.

Murmuring, grumbling and faultfinding — being negative — create an atmosphere where Satan can work, but worship does just the opposite. Some people carpool, and they grumble about something all the way to work. They gossip about people at work, complain about the boss or working conditions, and I can assure you that nothing at work will ever change because of their murmuring and grumbling unless it just gets worse.

Being grateful and thankful toward God begins to change us. We should thank God that we have a job; many people don't have one. I often thank God that I don't have to sleep on the streets and stand in a soup line to get my food. Concentrate on the things you do have, not the things you don't have.

> Enter into His gates with thanksgiving and a thank offering and into His courts with praise! Be thankful and say so to Him, bless and affectionately praise His name!
>
> PSALM 100:4

> I will bless the Lord at all times; His praise shall continually be in my mouth.
>
> PSALM 34:1

Worship transforms us. By starting to worship God for the changes that He is already working in us, we find that those changes start manifesting more and more, and we experience new levels of God's glory, which is the manifestation of all His excellencies. In other words, God will pour His goodness out upon the worshiper.

Don't forget the promises of God, the word He has spoken to You. While you're waiting for the manifestation you desire and God has promised, let your days and nights be filled with a positive attitude, praise, worship and thanksgiving.

If we forget God's Word to us, we begin to feel discouraged, defeated, impatient, negative and angry. What is in the heart comes out of the mouth, so naturally we begin to speak wrong things. God's Word teaches us that we get what we say. God calls things that don't exist yet as if they already existed. (Romans 4:17.) We should follow His example and do the same thing.

As we worship, we remain in position to receive.

Chapter 4

Phase 4 —
The Lord Brings Deliverance

And when they began to sing and to praise, the Lord set ambushments against the men of Ammon, Moab, and Mount Seir who had come against Judah, and they were [self-] slaughtered.

2 CHRONICLES 20:22

This verse says that while the people of Judah were singing praise to God, He set ambushments against their enemies, and the enemy slaughtered themselves. Praise confused the enemy.

I think this is the absolutely most awesome good news! Just think of it. They set themselves to seek God rather than live in fear. They told God how awesome He is; they stood and waited on God. He sent a prophet with a word for them, telling them the battle was not theirs but His. He told them to take their position and stand still. They worshiped and praised. Jehoshaphat appointed singers to sing and praise, and the Lord defeated their enemies by confusing them so much that they killed each other!

In Judges we see another example of God's deliverance through a battle plan that naturally would not seem to work.

Then Jerubbaal, that is, Gideon, and all the people who were with him rose early and encamped beside the spring of Harod;

and the camp of Midian was north of them by the hill of Moreh in the valley.

The Lord said to Gideon, The people who are with you are too many for Me to give the Midianites into their hands, lest Israel boast about themselves against Me, saying, My own hand has delivered me.

So now proclaim in the ears of the men, saying, Whoever is fearful and trembling, let him turn back and depart from Mount Gilead. And 22,000 of the men returned, but 10,000 remained.

JUDGES 7:1-3

Instead of telling Gideon, who was facing a major battle, that He would give him more men, God told him that he had too many for God to give him the victory. Interestingly enough, sometimes God works through our weaknesses better than through our strengths. There are times when we have too much going for us in the natural for God to give the victory. We are not in line for a miracle if anyone but God can help us. God was telling Gideon that they were too strong in themselves, that He wanted them in a position where they would have to depend entirely on Him.

Pride and boasting ruin the best of men so God has to help us stay humble and, under His mighty hand, totally dependent on Him. Israel has gone through the same thing over and over since their exodus from Egypt. They would lean entirely on God, and He would help them. Then they would become self-sufficient, disobedient and rebellious, thinking that they did not need God, and their circumstances would once again become bad. When they trusted God, they defeated their enemies; when they didn't, their enemies defeated them.

LET THE FEARFUL GO HOME

The Lord instructed Gideon to tell the men that those who were fearful should turn around and go home; 22,000 of them left, leaving 10,000 behind to face the enemy.

That tells us there were more men with fear than without. How many times does God put something on our heart to do, but then fear comes along, and we start to hesitate; we become double-minded? As I said previously, we may feel fear, but we can do it afraid if need be. God says "Fear not, for I am with you." This is the number one reason why we don't have to bow our knee to fear and let it control our destiny. God is with us and will protect us if we place our trust in Him.

> *And the Lord said to Gideon, The men are still too many; bring them down to the water, and I will test them for you there. And he of whom I say to you, This man shall go with you, shall go with you; and he of whom I say to you, This man shall not go with you, shall not go.*
>
> *So he brought the men down to the water, and the Lord said to Gideon, Everyone who laps up the water with his tongue as a dog laps it, you shall set by himself, likewise everyone who bows down on his knees to drink.*
>
> *And the number of those who lapped, putting their hand to their mouth, was 300 men, but all the rest of the people bowed down upon their knees to drink water.*
>
> *And the Lord said to Gideon, With the 300 men who lapped I will deliver you, and give the Midianites into your hand. Let all the others return every man to his home.*
>
> JUDGES 7:4-7

When I first read this passage, I thought, "What's all this lapping and bowing about?" I couldn't quite understand it, so I asked the Lord to show me what was behind it. He guided me to a footnote from another Bible I normally don't use that provides an explanation of this incident.

The scenario went something like this: The men of Gideon were all thirsty. When they saw the water, some of them ran to it, bowed down on their knees, put their face in the water and began to drink. Others just took their hands and cupped up the water, bringing it up to their mouth to drink. Those who cupped the water in their hands were able to still look around the area and watch out for the enemy while they were drinking. They remained alert and ready to do their real job while the others, the ones who bowed and put their face to the water, only thought about their immediate need while they forgot all about watching for the enemy.

The 300 who lapped the water showed wisdom and diligence. These are the type of people God chooses to work through.

RESIST ENTANGLEMENTS

When God gives us something to do, He places a call on our life. One of the things that we must not do is get so caught up in our own need that we stop doing what God has given us to do.

We have a tendency to get entangled in things. Paul told Timothy that no soldier in service got entangled with the things of civilian life. We must avoid entanglements with the world. We are in the world but must resist becoming worldly or loving the world and the things in it in an excessive manner.

Entanglements will get us off course and prevent us from completing the call of God on our lives. Sometimes we even get entangled in other people's problems. Although we certainly want to get involved and help people, we must not get out of balance. There is a difference between godly involvement and entanglements. We can even get entangled in our own needs. We can stay so busy trying to provide for ourselves that we miss God's will. In essence, that is what happed to the soldiers of Gideon who bowed and put their face in the water. They were so emotional about having their thirst quenched that they missed God's will for them. We must be on our guard against getting entangled and trapped.

> . . . let us strip off and throw aside every encumbrance (unnecessary weight) and that sin which so readily (deftly and cleverly) clings to and entangles us, and let us run with patient endurance and steady and active persistence the appointed course of the race that is set before us.
>
> HEBREWS 12:1

If you and I are going to do anything for God, we must resist entanglements. Let me give you an example:

At one time in the development of the ministry, we needed to buy some property and build a building for our ministry headquarters. It was going to be a long project and a mountain of work, but we had no choice. We either had to stifle our growth or build a building. We had looked for existing buildings for a long time so we could just move into one already finished, but we just could not find a suitable one that would also have some property for expansion when we needed it.

43

At first I resisted and resisted buying property and erecting a building because I knew it would be a lot of work, and I kept saying, "I don't want to get caught up in all that goes with building a building." I already had plenty to do and did not want to lose sight of my priorities, which are praying, studying, preaching, teaching and writing.

Although I am the type of person who naturally likes to be involved in whatever is going on, I told my husband, Dave, "I am not going to get entangled in developing the property, obtaining the building permits, drawing up blueprints and all of that. It is not what I am anointed to do." Dave is anointed for that type of thing and really enjoys it, so I had to discipline myself to stay out of it so I could give myself to my call.

When there is something that needs to be handled and it will take you away from your priority, look for somebody else and let them do it, or pay them to do it if you need to.

There were times when I almost had to get violent because I could feel the thing sucking me in. I had to keep saying to myself and other people, "I just cannot get entangled in this project." Of course there were some things I had to be involved in and didn't mind them, but I insisted on not going too far. It turned out to be a five-year project from beginning to end, and I am very thankful for our building. It is beautiful and paid for, which makes it even better.

Because I really did not want to get involved, occasionally I saw things being done, and I would think, "I don't like that." But then I had to remind myself, or Dave would remind me, that I chose not to be involved to any great degree, so I should realize everything might not be exactly as I would have done it. Not becoming entangled with the project over the five-year span was worth having to put up with a few (very few) things I didn't care for.

I have discovered that I can either do everything myself and have a life filled with stress and pressure, or I can trust others and give them authority. There are more ways to do things than my way. We might all get to the same place by a different route, but it doesn't matter that much, as long as we arrive at our destination. I encourage you to empower people to help you, but don't give them responsibility without authority. If you do, it will frustrate them, and ultimately they will not be able to do what you really wanted them to do.

Whatever needs to be done in our lives, there are people who are anointed for it. Actually, if we don't allow them to do the part God sent them to do, they become frustrated and so do we.

When the time came to decorate the building, I got very involved, but it was a short-term project and something I enjoyed. I stayed out of the rest of it, and my husband did an outstanding job.

We should all occasionally take an inventory of our activities, and make sure we are giving ourselves to our priorities. If we find we have become entangled in something that is not bearing fruit for us or God, we need to readjust and get back to letting the main thing be the main thing.

KEEP YOUR EYES ON GOD

So the people took provisions and their trumpets in their hands, and he sent all the rest of Israel every man to his home and retained those 300 men. And the host of Midian was below him in the valley.

That same night the Lord said to Gideon, Arise, go down against their camp, for I have given it into your hand.

But if you fear to go down, go with Purah your servant down to the camp

And you shall hear what they say, and afterward your hands shall be strengthened to go down against the camp. Then he went down with Purah his servant to the outposts of the camp of the armed men.

And the Midanites and the Amalekites and all the sons of the east lay along the valley like locusts for multitude; and their camels were without number, as the sand on the seashore for multitude.

When Gideon arrived, behold, a man was telling a dream to his comrade. And he said, Behold, I dreamed a dream, and behold, a cake of barley bread tumbled into the camp of Midian and came to the tent and struck it so that it fell, and turned it upside down so that the tent lay flat.

JUDGES 7:8-13

Here we see Gideon receiving the word he needed from God — only this time it is coming through a dream. Gideon needed such an encouraging word because out of an army of 32,000 men, he was left with only 300. The opposing army was a large multitude whose camp spread so far that it looked like the sands of the sea. The dream was letting Gideon know that the enemy's camp would be flattened and destroyed by supernatural means.

The footnote of the reference to the barley bread (verse 13) in *The Amplified Bible* says: "Alluding to the insignificance of Gideon and his family, or perhaps his whole troop. Barley then, as it is still, was distinguished from 'fine flour.'" The footnote includes a quote from Bishop Joseph Hall that is cited by *The Cambridge Bible* (we have modernized the spelling): "To hear himself but a Barley-cake, troubled him not. It matters not how base we be thought, so we be victorious."

This should encourage us that we don't need much in the natural to win our battles. We don't need to inventory our natural resources. All we need to do is keep our eyes on God.

God showed Gideon that as an insignificant barley cake could be used to flatten the camp of the enemy, so he could be used also. The Lord was not trying to insult Gideon. He was trying to get him in the place that all of us must be in — knowing that without God, he could do nothing.

GET THE WORD AND WORSHIP

And his comrade replied, This is nothing else but the sword of Gideon son of Joash, a man of Israel. Into his hand God has given Midian and all the host.

When Gideon heard the telling of the dream and its interpretation, he worshiped and returned to the camp of Israel and said, Arise, for the Lord has given into your hand the host of Midian.

JUDGES 7:14,15

As soon as Gideon received that personal word from God, he began to talk about the battle as if it were already won. He began to praise and worship God as if the victory were already an accomplished fact. He didn't wait to see the results of the battle before he proclaimed the triumph of the Lord.

47

I am still amazed to see how often the people whom God used stopped to worship. It has taught me a great lesson, and I pray that it will have the same effect on you as you read this book. We must not be like the lepers who asked for healing, yet 90 percent of them had no time to stop and give praise. Only one out of ten came back to give thanks. Jesus said, . . . **but where are the nine?** In others words, He notices when we fail to worship Him.

In the book of Exodus, the Israelites sang the right song after they had passed through the Red Sea while their enemies had been drowned: . . . **the horse and its rider He** [the Lord] **has thrown into the sea** (Exodus 15:1 NKJV). But they sang it on the wrong side of the river. They were all excited. They had their tambourines out and were singing and dancing. They went into a long dissertation about the greatness of God. But it was *after* they had seen the manifestation of His power. They sang the right song but on the wrong side of the river.

It would certainly be a tragedy not to praise and worship after victories, but Gideon did the right thing in worshiping before. He had only *heard* about the victory from God, and he started worshiping. This kind of behavior is going the extra mile, and it gets the attention of God.

I believe we see why the Israelites wandered in the wilderness for so long by looking at their pattern of worship. If they had sung the right song in the midst of the wilderness, they would not have had to stay out there forty years. They would probably have been through the Red Sea and living in the Promised Land in about two weeks. It is actually recorded in Deuteronomy that it took them forty long years to make an eleven-day journey.

I have been enlightened to see how many people came to Jesus for healing, bowing down and worshiping Him before asking for anything.

When Jesus came down from the mountain, great throngs followed Him.

And behold, a leper came up to Him and, prostrating himself, worshiped Him, saying, Lord, if You are willing, You are able to cleanse me by curing me.

And He reached out His hand and touched him, saying, I am willing; be cleansed by being cured. And instantly his leprosy was cured and cleansed.

MATTHEW 8:1-3

And behold, a woman who was a Canaanite from that district came out and, with a [loud, troublesomely urgent] cry, begged, Have mercy on me, O Lord, Son of David! My daughter is miserably and distressingly and cruelly possessed by a demon!

But He did not answer her a word. And His disciples came and implored Him, saying, Send her away, for she is crying out after us.

He answered, I was sent only to the lost sheep of the house of Israel.

But she came and, kneeling, worshiped Him and kept praying, Lord, help me!

And He answered, It is not right (proper, becoming, or fair) to take the children's bread and throw it to the little dogs.

She said, Yes, Lord, yet even the little pups (little whelps) eat the crumbs that fall from their [young] masters' table.

Then Jesus answered her, O woman, great is your faith! Be it done for you as you wish. And her daughter was cured from that moment.

MATTHEW 15:22-28

And when they approached the multitude, a man came up to Him, kneeling before Him and saying,

Lord, do pity and have mercy on my son, for he has epilepsy (is moonstruck) and he suffers terribly; for frequently he falls into the fire and many times into the water.

And I brought him to Your disciples, and they were not able to cure him.

And Jesus answered, O you unbelieving (warped, wayward, rebellious) and thoroughly perverse generation! How long am I to remain with you? How long am I to bear with you? Bring him here to Me.

And Jesus rebuked the demon, and it came out of him, and the boy was cured instantly.

MATTHEW 17:14-18

We continue seeing, through all these examples, that worship comes *before* victory.

LET THE LORD FIGHT THE BATTLE

And he divided the 300 men into three companies, and he put into the hands of all of them trumpets and empty pitchers, with torches inside the pitchers.

And he said to them, Look at me, then do likewise. When I come to the edge of their camp, do as I do.

When I blow the trumpet, I and all who are with me, then you blow the trumpets also on every side of all the camp and shout, For the Lord and for Gideon!

So Gideon and the 100 men who were with him came to the outskirts of the camp at the beginning of the middle watch, when the guards had just been changed, and they blew the trumpets and smashed the pitchers that were in their hands.

And the three companies blew the trumpets and shattered the pitchers, holding the torches in their left hands, and in their right hands the trumpets to blow [leaving no chance to use swords], and they cried, The sword for the Lord and Gideon!

JUDGES 7:16-20

Notice the phrase **leaving no chance to use swords**. When God sent each man of the tiny army of Gideon out to do battle with a vastly superior host of Midianites, He purposely put something in both hands of each man so that the man could not help himself — he could not draw his sword and begin to fight his own battle. God sent out 300 men who were fearless and focused on what they were called to do, and He sent them with something in each hand so they could not possibly fight their own battle — they had to depend on Him to fight it for them. All they had to do was break a pitcher, hold up a torch and cry, **The sword for the Lord and Gideon!** In other words, all they had to do was hold forth the light and praise the Lord.

The instructions to Gideon were different from those to Jehoshaphat. That is why we must hear from God each time for ourselves. We cannot just do what someone else did. Even though it worked for them, it will not always work for us.

WHAT HAPPENED

They stood every man in his place round about the camp, and all the [Midianite] army ran — they cried out and fled.

When [Gideon's men] blew the 300 trumpets, the Lord set every [Midianite's] sword against his comrade and against all the army, and the army fled. . . .

JUDGES 7:21,22

What happened was the same thing that happened with Jehoshaphat. When the army of the Lord did what God told them to do, the way God told them to do it, the enemy began to slaughter themselves.

Once again God's battle plan when put into action by faith was totally successful.

Part

2

Transformed through Worship

Chapter

5

Elijah Stayed in Position

Elijah was a human being with a nature such as we have [with feelings, affections, and a constitution like ours]; and he prayed earnestly for it not to rain, and no rain fell on the earth for three years and six months.

And [then] he prayed again and the heavens supplied rain and the land produced its crops [as usual].

JAMES 5:17,18

In 1 Kings 17:1 Elijah, the prophet of the Lord, told wicked King Ahab that no rain would fall on the land of Israel during those years, but it would be according to the word of the Lord.

During all that time of drought, God took care of Elijah. First, He hid him by the brook Cherith and sent ravens to bring him food. (Verses 2-6.) Then, when the brook dried up and there was no water for Elijah to drink, God sent him to Zarephath to the home of a poor widow, where He miraculously provided for Elijah, the widow and her young son until He decided to send rain upon the land once more. (Verses 7-24.)

After these years, the Lord sent Elijah back to King Ahab to tell him it was about to rain again. Ahab was a very wicked man, and where there is wickedness there will always be drought and famine of some kind. When people are not serving God, they are always going to experience lack, both spiritually and physically.

ELIJAH'S MESSAGE TO AHAB

And Elijah said to Ahab, Go up, eat and drink, for there is the sound of abundance of rain.

1 KINGS 18:41

God had brought drought and famine on Israel to show His power to Ahab. He was letting Ahab and his wicked wife, Jezebel, know that they needed to change their wicked ways, and if they didn't, the circumstances were not going to be good.

After three years of famine, He sent His prophet Elijah to show himself to Ahab and tell him it was going to rain.

So Elijah went and told Ahab, "You had better get ready because I hear the sound of an abundance of rain. You had better get prepared because there is going to be a downpour."

Ahab and Jezebel could not stand the sight of Elijah because he was a prophet and servant of God. Have you ever noticed how wicked people hate you for no reason at all that you can find? They will hate you just because you represent the One they are rebelling against. Elijah showed himself to Ahab, and that alone was enough to put Ahab in a rage. Although Ahab wanted rain, he did not want Elijah to be right or to be the one who seemed to be in control.

I don't believe Elijah really heard the sound of rain in the natural. He heard it in the spirit by faith, but not in the natural.

He was listening to the Spirit of God; he believed what He said and began to act on it *before* he saw the manifestation of it.

ANNOUNCE IT TO THE DEVIL

Just as Elijah announced, or prophesied, to wicked King Ahab that it was going to rain, so we need to announce to the devil what is going to happen in our life according to the Word of God.

Say things like: "Satan, I will tell you right now, you may come against me one way, but you are going to flee before me seven ways. Right now it may look to you like you have won the victory, but you have made a serious mistake. You have picked on the wrong person. I belong to God, and He takes care of His own."

Some time ago my husband, Dave, and I encountered a time when we had multiple trials coming against us all at the same time. One day Dave came in and announced, "The devil may think he is having a heyday, but soon he is going to be calling, 'Mayday, Mayday.'"

That is the attitude and position we should all have when we face the enemy and his attacks against us. Instead of listening to Satan tell us all the terrible things that are going to happen to us, we should start announcing to him all the good things God has planned for our lives and all the terrible things that are going to happen to him.

When the Lord decided it was time to send rain on the earth again, the first thing He did was send His prophet Elijah to announce to King Ahab what He was about to do for His people.

You need to make an announcement to "Ahab," that is, to the devil. Don't go announce to all your friends what the devil has done to you; announce to him what God is going to do for you and to him. Remind Satan that God is just and that He will bring justice in your life; He will make everything that is wrong, right. Let him know that if he hangs around you, all he is going to hear is singing, laughing, the Word of God, praise, worship and thanksgiving.

Learn to talk back to the devil. He stays busy talking to us, but when we start talking back, he will shut up!

HOLD YOUR POSITION

. . . And Elijah went up to the top of Carmel; and he bowed himself down upon the earth and put his face between his knees

And said to his servant, Go up now, look toward the sea. And he went up and looked and said, There is nothing. Elijah said, Go again seven times.

And at the seventh time the servant said, A cloud as small as a man's hand is arising out of the sea. And Elijah said, Go up, say to Ahab, Hitch your chariot and go down, lest the rain stop you.

In a little while, the heavens were black with wind-swept clouds, and there was a great rain. . . .

1 KINGS 18:42-45

After announcing to Ahab what was going to happen, that there was coming an abundance of rain, Elijah went up to the top of Mount Carmel. There he got down on his knees with his forehead on the ground.

In that position of worship, Elijah sent his servant to run back and forth several times to see if it was starting to rain.

Seven times his servant came back with a bad report, but never did Elijah get out of that position. Just imagine how Elijah must have felt every time the report came back that nothing was happening: "There's not even a cloud out there." But each time Elijah just said, "Go again." Despite the repeated negative reports, Elijah never gave up. All he did was stay right where he was — worshiping God.

Worship strengthens our faith. Doubt may have caused Elijah to give up, but his worship kept him strong. Romans 4 tells us that Abraham had absolutely no human reason to hope. Doubt and unbelief came against him, but it did not defeat him. He became strong as he gave praise and glory to God. The same thing (praise and worship) seems to work for everyone we read about in the Bible; therefore, we certainly can believe it will work for us also.

Elijah's servant may have been saying to him, "Elijah, you must have missed God this time because nothing is happening; there's not even a cloud out there." But each time Elijah just said, "Go again." He refused to give up!

Finally, Elijah's servant came back and reported to him, "Well, I do see one small cloud about the size of a man's hand."

At that word, up came Elijah shouting, "Hallelujah! Go tell Ahab to hurry home and seek shelter because it's beginning to rain!"

When you worship God, He will send a Holy Ghost rain upon you, and it will drown all the "Ahabs" and all the "-ites" in your life. Just take your position and praise the Lord, giving Him all the glory before you ever see a change, as well as after your breakthrough.

If you will do that, if you will take the word from the Lord that you receive from this book and apply it in your life consistently, I can assure you that you will be blessed and see positive changes in your life. If you want to be victorious over all the power of the enemy, learn to follow God's marvelous battle plan.

Chapter

6

Don't Wrestle — Worship

For we are not wrestling with flesh and blood. . . .

EPHESIANS 6:12

In waging spiritual warfare, we must remember that we war against Satan and his demons, not against flesh and blood — that is, not against other people.

I would like to add that not only is our war not with the people around us, it is also not with our own selves.

Probably the greatest war we wage is one we wage with ourselves about ourselves, struggling with where we are spiritually compared to where we see we need to be. We may struggle with thinking that we need to have accomplished more in life than we have; we may feel like a financial failure or many other things. But one thing is a fact: We won't change anything by being frustrated and struggling. Remember, only God can fight our battles and win. These types of battles are different, but they are battles nonetheless, and must be handled the same way the rest of our battles are.

It is very difficult to get to the place where we can be honest with ourselves about our sin and failures, our inabilities and fallibilities, and yet still know that we are right with God because Jesus made us right when He died for us and rose from the dead.

Who we are in Christ is different from what we do in action and must be looked at two different ways.

Salvation is our most awesome blessing. Yet I feel that there are many Christians who will make it to heaven because they are born again but will never truly enjoy the journey because they have never learned to enjoy themselves and God.

The reason they never enjoy themselves is because they are in a private internal war with themselves about all their deficiencies. The reason they never enjoy God is because most of the time they vaguely feel that God is displeased with them, even angry with them, because of their flaws. They are always wrestling with themselves, always in a war, always struggling.

If you are at war with yourself, this word from the Lord is especially for you.

Are You a Trial to Yourself?

I once did a teaching titled "Have you become a trial to yourself?"

We are always talking about our many trials, but often our greatest trial is with ourselves. We have more trouble with us than we do with the devil or any person on earth.

Earlier in this book we discussed the power of worship. Here, we are going to continue to examine that same subject, specifically how we can be changed as we worship God and behold God — not as we look to ourselves, adding up our many flaws — but as we look to Him.

<u>We Are Changing</u>

But we all, with open face beholding as in a glass the glory of the Lord, are changed into the same image from glory to glory, even as by the Spirit of the Lord.

2 Corinthians 3:18 kjv

I want to change, and I am sure you do also. I want to see changes in my behavior. I want to see regular progress. For example, I want more stability; I want to walk in a greater measure of love and all the other fruit of the Spirit. I want to be kind and good to others, even if I don't feel good or am not having a particularly good day. Even when things are coming against me and I am not getting my way in life, I still want to be stable and display the character of Jesus Christ.

We cannot do it on our own, but we have been given the Helper, the Holy Spirit Himself, to aid us in our endeavors to be like Jesus. Remember, we cannot do anything on our own.

Through the power of the Holy Spirit within us, we are able to be sweet, nice and kind, even when things are not going our way. We are able to stay calm when everything around us seems topsy-turvy, when everything seems to be conspiring against us to cause us to lose our patience and get angry and upset.

Some years ago our youngest son got his driver's license. We had helped him get a car, and it had been in the garage waiting for him even before he could drive, so he was very anxious to get started driving on his own.

Actually, like any other young person, he had plans to drive his car somewhere the first night he got his license. He wanted to drive to a home Bible study group he was involved in, in another area of town. It was a long distance, and Dave told him that he did not want him to take it there because it was snowing outside.

He asked if he could come home and get it and go out after the Bible study, and we said he could probably do that. However, it was snowing even harder by the time he got home, and once again, he had to face disappointment as we told him he could not take the car out.

He had a friend stay overnight that evening, and they had plans to get up early the next morning and take the car out. By the time Dave got up and dressed, the boys already had the car in the driveway, making preparation to leave. Dave had to go somewhere, and he left ahead of them. As he got out on the roads, he realized that they were really slippery from the snow, and, in fact, it was still snowing. Dave called me and told me to tell Danny that he could not take the car out. I did not really want to be the bearer of the bad news, so I took the phone to Danny and let his dad tell him he had to stay home. Of course, Danny was very disappointed and, at that point, got angry. He wanted to do what he wanted to do, even though deep down inside I am sure he realized it wasn't very wise.

I told you this story because that is our normal reaction when we don't get our way. Our emotions get stirred up and begin flying in all directions.

I told Danny to just stay sweet. I said, "This is only one day in your life. You will have lots of other days to drive your car." I tried to tell him about how God tests us and stretches us through those tests, often preparing us for future blessings. My encouragement didn't seem to help very much, but I know exactly how he felt because I have been there hundreds of times myself, and you probably have also.

One of my personal goals is to stay sweet, even when I don't get my way. I have improved a lot over the years, but I can testify that I did not make any positive progress until I learned that I could not change myself. I had to go to God and take my position of waiting on and worshiping Him and learn He would fight the battle for me.

I needed a great deal of change. I was sexually, mentally and emotionally abused during my childhood, and I had many problems as a result of that treatment. I was rebellious toward authority, especially male authority. I had a bad attitude. I didn't trust people. I felt sorry for myself. I had a chip on my shoulder, among many other problems, and I felt as if the world owed me something.

Don't spend your life trying to collect what is due you from someone who can never pay you back. God says He will be our Vindicator, our Reward and our Recompense. He actually promises to give us double blessings for our former trouble, but we must place our trust in Him and not try to make things happen ourselves.

Yes, I had lots of problems, but as I look back over the years, I have changed a lot. My husband, Dave, would readily testify to that. When we first got married in 1966, if he made me angry, I might not speak a word to him for two or three weeks. Now I cannot stand to stay angry for more than a few minutes. I grew up in a home where everyone was controlled with anger and fear, so it was the only way I knew to react when I didn't get what I wanted. But God taught me new ways to act and react.

I changed, but not until I first suffered many years wrestling with myself — not liking myself, feeling like God was angry with me and displeased. I felt guilty and condemned all the time; it actually was very tormenting. I was literally never relaxed.

I really tried to change but had very little to no results, and then I finally learned about God's grace and that He changed us through His grace, not through our struggle.

When I look back over the years, I realize I have come a long way, but it happened little by little. That is how God changes us. He reveals something to us and then waits until we decide to trust Him with it before He works in us His character in that area.

The amount of time the changes require is dependent on 1) how long it takes us to get into agreement with God that we do have the problem He says we have; 2) how long it takes us to stop making excuses and blaming it on someone else; 3) how long we spin our wheels, so to speak, trying to change ourselves; 4) how much time we spend studying His Word, waiting on and worshiping Him, truly believing that He is working in us all the while we seek Him.

God is always trying to work in us, in our families and circumstances. He is ever present. He calls Himself "I AM." He is not "I Was" or "I Will Be" but "I AM," present right now and ready to work in our lives. He is a gentleman and will not force His way into our lives; He must be invited. As we relax under His mighty hand, He begins to remold us into what His original intention was before the world messed us up. He will definitely do a good job, if we will release ourselves into His mighty hand.

Releasing God

We release God to work as we release our faith. God can change you while you read this book, if you will trust Him to do so. He will work on both you and your situation while you sit in His Presence and enjoy Him.

We struggle and work so hard trying to change ourselves. Sometimes we get mad at ourselves and even hate ourselves because of the way we are.

Our younger daughter, Sandra, was dramatically and permanently changed the first time she heard me teach the message "The Battle Belongs to the Lord." She realized that she was not trusting God to change her at all. She was angry at herself much of the time for her imperfections, but that anger came out of her in a way that made others think she was angry with them. She hated the bad temper, the anger and the upset, but she seemed powerless to change until she heard the message.

She testifies that she began crying almost uncontrollably as she heard the message in the conference where I first preached it. She realized that she was not worshiping God or trusting Him; instead, she wanted to change herself so she could feel good about it and be proud. She got a mighty release that evening and has applied these principles ever since, with good results.

Some people become consumed by the desire to be seen as perfect. They hate themselves every time they make a mistake. This self-hatred and self-rejection become major problems. This attitude not only causes problems in them and their relationship with God, but it also causes problems in relationships with other people. All of our relationships begin with the foundation of how we feel about ourselves. If we don't get along with ourselves, we won't get along with anyone else either.

I believe that one of my roles as a teacher and author is not only to help people change, but also to help them learn how to enjoy where they are on the way to where they are going. In fact, I have written an entire book on the subject. To obtain a copy see the book list in the back of this book.

I think the greatest tragedy in life is to live and not enjoy life. If you are warring with yourself all the time, you are not enjoying your life. Since the Bible says that we war not against flesh and blood, your war is not with yourself. It is with demonic principalities and powers that have gained strongholds in your life through deception in years past. Those deceptions are being uncovered on a regular basis by the truth in God's Word. The Bible says that the truth will set us free if we continue in it. Stick with God's battle plan, and you will like the results.

God changes us from one degree of glory to another, but don't forget to enjoy the glory you are in right now while you are headed for the next one. Don't compare the glory you are in with the glory of some friend or family member who appears to be in a greater degree of glory. Each of us is an individual, and God deals with us differently, according to what He knows we need and can handle.

You may not notice changes on a daily basis, but as you look back over the years, you will see very definite changes in yourself. I want to stir your faith up so even when you don't seem to see changes, you will believe that God is working, just like He said He would. We must be like Elijah and refuse to give up until we see results. When the devil or even friends tell us we are not changing, we should just continue to wait on and worship God and ignore their discouraging report.

Remember, we see *after* we believe, not *before*. We wrestle and struggle with ourselves because of all that we are not, when we should be praising and worshiping God for all that we are. As we worship Him for Who He is, we see things released into our lives that we could have never made happen ourselves.

As we worship God, we are released from frustration. All those pent-up, weird, emotional things that need to go begin to vanish. As we worship, God's character is released into our lives and begins to manifest.

One of my struggles was with being gentle. I was more of a harsh, hard, pressing person. I could ask someone to take out the trash and end up sounding like a strict army sergeant giving orders. I didn't want to be that way, but no matter how hard I tried to change, people were always asking me why I had to sound so strict and harsh.

I was treated that way growing up so I became that way. As I studied God's character, I learned He was not that way, and I certainly didn't want to be that way either, but I couldn't change. The reason I couldn't change was because I was trying to change myself. I was not trusting God to do it. I had become an achiever instead of a believer.

Every day I had my plan, and when my plan didn't work (which was all the time), then I would be angrier with myself than I was the day before. So in some instances, for me, learning the Word of God actually was torment. Before I began studying God's Word, I had problems but didn't know it. I thought everyone else had a problem, not me. After studying God's

Word, I learned that I had problems and lots of them, but still I was powerless to change until, as I continued studying God's Word, I discovered His battle plan. That is why we must *continue* in the Word of God if we want to be set free.

If I had given up too soon and not continued in the Word, I would have been a very miserable person. Thank God that even when we want to give up, He won't let us. He remains faithful, even when we are faithless. (2 Timothy 2:13.)

As I said, when we worship God for His attributes, they are released into our lives. One of those attributes happens to be gentleness. Guess what? As I worshiped God for Who He was, I changed, and I am not harsh any longer.

If you are not the way you want to be in some area of your life, begin to worship God in that area. As you worship Him for any of the attributes of His character — His faithfulness, His loyalty, His goodness, His kindness, His love, His graciousness, His longsuffering, His slowness to anger, His plenteousness in mercy, His patience — whatever you worship Him for will begin to be manifested in your own character.

Our Goal: Christlikeness

For those whom He foreknew [of whom He was aware and loved beforehand], He also destined from the beginning [foreordaining them] to be molded into the image of His Son [and share inwardly His likeness], that He might become the firstborn among many brethren.

ROMANS 8:29

Our number one goal in life as Christians should be Christlikeness. Jesus is the express image of the Father, and we are to follow in His footsteps. He came as the Pioneer of our faith to show us by example how we should live and conduct ourselves.

We should seek to behave with people the way Jesus did. Our goal is not to see how successful we can be in business or how famous we can be. It is not prosperity, popularity or even building a big ministry, but to be Christlike.

The world doesn't only need a sermon preached to them; they also need to see actions backing up what we say we believe as Christians. Our lives should make other people hungry and thirsty for what we have in Christ. The Bible refers to us as **salt**, which makes people thirsty, and **light**, which exposes darkness.

Many Christians have bumper stickers on their car, or they wear some kind of jewelry that indicates they are a believer in Jesus Christ. The world is not impressed by our bumper stickers and Christian jewelry; they want to see fruit of godly behavior.

They want to see people who claim to be Christians living what they preach, not just preaching to others while it doesn't seem to be working in their own lives.

The Bible speaks to us about change. If we will let Him, God changes us from glory to glory as we study His Word. We see His image in the written Word of God, and it becomes as a mirror to us. In other words, we see ourselves in light of the Bible and realize we need to change.

As we begin praying about the changes we need and desire and seek God for them, little by little He changes us to be more and more like Him.

I often see bumper stickers that say, "Please be patient with me; God isn't finished with me yet." Actually, He is finished; His work was finished when He died on the cross. We just need to believe it and, thereby, receive it. Spiritually speaking, His work was finished, but experientially it is being worked out in our lives daily.

The Bible says that the One Who began a good work in us will bring it to full completion.

> *And I am convinced and sure of this very thing, that He Who began a good work in you will continue until the day of Jesus Christ [right up to the time of His return], developing [that good work] and perfecting and bringing it to full completion in you.*
>
> PHILIPPIANS 1:6

When I say we need to be Christlike, I am speaking of a goal we pursue. We don't have to be perfect to be a witness to others, but neither can we expect to be carnal or fleshly and impress them with our faith.

What we pursue in life is very important. I am concerned that sometimes as Christians we continue pursuing what the world pursues except we put a Christian label on it.

Here is an example:

I am a very goal-oriented person, one with vision and purpose. I was voted the girl most likely to succeed in high school. In 1976, when God touched my life and filled me with the Holy Spirit, I entered a very serious and committed relationship with the Lord. I had accepted Jesus as my Savior when I was nine years old. In my twenties I began going to church regularly and did a lot of church-oriented things. We belonged to all the right clubs; we were involved and sat on various church boards; yet, to be honest, my life was not very different from the the lives of unbelievers I knew and worked with.

After receiving the baptism of the Holy Spirit and receiving a call into ministry, I made a deeper commitment, but several years went by before I realized I was still pursuing wrong things. I wanted to be successful in ministry; I wanted my life to be blessed, but I wasn't pursuing Christlikeness with all my heart.

I did have a desire to change, but I wanted it to "just happen." I was not ready to pay the price I would need to pay to have spiritual maturity.

THE PRICE TO PAY

So, since Christ suffered in the flesh for us, for you, arm yourselves with the same thought and purpose [patiently to suffer rather than fail to please God]. For whoever has suffered in the flesh [having the mind of Christ] is done with [intentional] sin [has stopped pleasing himself and the world, and pleases God],

So that he can no longer spend the rest of his natural life living by [his] human appetites and desires, but [he lives] for what God wills.

1 PETER 4:1,2

"Sacrifice" and "suffering" are not always popular words among Christians, but nonetheless, they are biblical words and ones that Jesus and the apostles frequently talked about. Spiritual maturity or "Christlikeness" cannot be obtained without "dying to self."

That simply means saying yes to God and no to ourselves when our will and God's are in opposition.

Paul spoke of dying daily. He said things like, "It is no longer I who live, but Christ Who lives in me." Jesus told His disciples that if they wanted to follow Him, they would need to take up their cross daily. *The Amplified Bible* brings a clear definition concerning this cross Jesus speaks of.

> *And Jesus called [to Him] the throng with His disciples and said to them, If anyone intends to come after Me, let him deny himself [forget, ignore, disown, and lose sight of himself and his own interests] and take up his cross, and [joining Me as a disciple and siding with My party] follow with Me [continually, cleaving steadfastly to Me].*
>
> MARK 8:34

To follow Christ and become like Him, we must be willing to forget all about what we want — our plans, having our own way — and instead trust Him to show us what His will is for us.

His will always leads to deep joy and satisfaction, but it takes some time in our life and experience for us to realize that. In the beginning, when we start giving up things and allowing God-inspired changes in our life, we suffer in the flesh. In other words, our flesh has a mind of its own, and it does not want to give up its plan. It doesn't want to sacrifice, be uncomfortable, inconvenienced or even to wait.

First Peter 4, quoted above, states that we must have **the mind of Christ** Who **suffered in the flesh for us.** In other words, we must think, "I would rather suffer in the will of God than suffer out of God's will." When we are willing to pay the price and suffer to be in God's will, it is a type of suffering that leads to glorious victory, a type that eventually goes away. But if we remain out of God's will, we will endure a type of misery and suffering that never goes away.

When I speak of suffering, I am not referring to poverty, disease and disaster. I am speaking of the suffering the flesh goes through when it does not get its own way. The flesh is composed of the soul — mind, will, emotions — and body, or our own ways of being and doing. We have all of these, but we are first and foremost a spiritual being, and we are called by God to walk in the Spirit. This simply means we are to follow the guidance of the Holy Spirit, Who dwells inside the human spirit of the believer in Christ. The Holy Spirit is to be the Guide and leading factor in our Christian lives because He will guide us into all truth and into God's perfect will.

I highly exhort you to be willing to pay the price; the prize is well worth it!

Chapter

7

Be Transfigured

The Bible talks about transformation and transfiguration. In Luke chapter 9 Jesus was transfigured. He went up into a mountain to pray; Peter and John were with him. As He was praying, the appearance of His countenance became altered. It changed, and His garments became dazzling white. Moses and Elijah were conversing with Him, speaking to Him of His exit from life, which would soon come to pass. Of course, Peter and John were astonished; they had never witnessed anything like it before. Peter wanted to build booths and just remain on the mountain forever; however, Jesus told him that they had to go back down the mountain and be with the other people.

Peter, John and Jesus went up on the mountain, and they all witnessed this great event. Jesus wanted to go back down and minister to the people; Peter wanted to stay there and just keep enjoying himself the rest of his life.

Notice that Jesus was transfigured **as He was praying.** Although the Bible does not expressly say that He was worshiping, I believe Jesus always worshiped when He prayed. I certainly believe His prayers contained more praise than petition. This is a lesson for all of us. If we want to see positive change in our lives, let's pray, praise and worship instead of building booths. We are often so busy trying to build our own thing, we don't even realize the great work God wants to do and His purpose in doing it. God does not want us to become

Christlike just so we can enjoy our lives more. He wants us to spend time with Him in prayer and the Word, experience trans-figuration, go back where the people are and help them in a greater way.

CHANGE THE COURSE OF YOUR DAY

If you get up in the morning in a terrible mood, the best thing you can do is find a place and spend some time with the Lord. Being in His Presence transforms us. We can change the course of a day that Satan has negative plans for by learning to seek God quickly when we sense any attitude or behavior that is not Christlike.

Apart from Him, we can do nothing (John 15:5), but with and through Him, we can do all things. (Philippians 4:13.) I have learned that I will always have feelings, but I don't have to let them rule me. I can't override them on my own, but if I seek God for help, He will strengthen me to walk in His Spirit, not in my emotions.

What if someone offends us or hurts our feelings? The Bible says we are not to be easily offended or touchy; we are all commanded to quickly forgive those who hurt us.

We may want to do what is right but find the doing of it difficult. That is when we need to take time to pray, spend some time with God, go to His Word and let our hearts meditate on a few Scriptures that deal with what we are going through. As a result, you and I will find strength to do the right thing.

Remember, we are in a war; we are soldiers in God's army, and we must be ready at any time to use our weapons. Some of those weapons are prayer, worship, praise and the Word of God.

WATCH YOUR COUNTENANCE

And the Lord said to Moses,

Say to Aaron and his sons, This is the way you shall bless the Israelites. Say to them,

The Lord bless you and watch, guard, and keep you;

The Lord make His face to shine upon and enlighten you and be gracious (kind, merciful, and giving favor) to you;

The Lord lift up His [approving] countenance upon you and give you peace (tranquility of heart and life continually).

NUMBERS 6:22-26

Jesus' countenance was changed on the mountain as He was transfigured. Our countenance is simply the way we look. It refers to our face. In the church today we need to be concerned about our countenance.

One of the blessings that was pronounced upon God's people was that God's face would shine upon them and that He would lift up His countenance upon them.

When the world looks at us, they need to see something about us that is different from them. They can't read our minds or see into our hearts, so our countenance is the only way we can show them that we have something they do not have but really want and need.

When Jesus began to pray and commune with God the Father, His countenance was changed, and we need the same thing to happen to us.

It is important what our countenance is like. It is important the look we have on our face at work. It is important the voice tone we use with our family at home. It is important that we smile at one another, that we are pleasant and just downright nice to each other.

I believe that we look better when we worship God. Worship puts a smile on our face. It is very hard to keep a scowl on our face while we are being thankful, praising and worshiping God. If we regularly do these things, our countenance will carry His Presence, not the expression of inner frustration and turmoil.

Perhaps we need to take a course in what I will call "faceology." We need to spend more time worshiping God, then our face would carry His glory.

Christians are supposed to be joyful people who walk in love. We must ask ourselves, "Would people know that I am a Christian by looking at my countenance most of the time?" I remember once when I was part of a conference in Florida. I walked into the building in the morning and proceeded down a corridor, when a woman spoke to me. I said hello in response to her greeting, and she said, "I can tell you have been with Jesus."

She was right. I had spent a long time that morning in prayer and fellowship with the Lord, preparing for the teaching I would do that day. How could she tell I had been with Jesus? Something about my countenance let her know. Perhaps I looked happy and satisfied, or peaceful. I don't know exactly what she saw, but something about the look on my face let her know Who I was spending my time with.

More Praise than Petition

When Jesus came down from the mountain, great throngs followed Him.

And behold, a leper came up to Him and, prostrating himself, worshiped Him, saying, Lord, if You are willing, You are able to cleanse me by curing me.

And He reached out His hand and touched him, saying, I am willing; be cleansed by being cured. And instantly his leprosy was cured and cleansed.

MATTHEW 8:1-3

We don't deal with leprosy in America where I am from, but there are still countries where leprosy exists today. While we may not deal with physical leprosy here in our day, we surely deal with a lot of spiritual leprosy.

So often we go to God for healing, breakthrough or deliverance, and what we want or need is the first thing we talk to Him about: "Lord, I need healing. I can't stand this pain anymore. You've got to do something, Lord; You've got to change my circumstance."

But when this man came to Jesus for healing of his leprosy, he first prostrated himself before Him and worshiped Him. Then he asked, "Lord, would You please heal me?"

There is a strong message here that we may have overlooked: Worshiping needs to come before asking. In our prayers, there needs to be more praise than petition.

It is fine to ask God for things. The Bible teaches us to do so, but I don't believe it is where we should start our conversation with God. What we start talking about first probably shows what is the most important thing to us.

I was once challenged by the Lord to examine closely the apostle Paul's prayers, several of which are recorded in the Bible. I was not only amazed at what I found, but I was convicted that my priority in prayer was not what it should be.

Paul prayed in Ephesians for the people to know and experience the love of God, to have a real revelation concerning the power of God available to them. In Philippians he prayed for them to choose excellent things. In Colossians he prayed that the people would be strengthened with all power to exercise every kind of endurance and patience with joy. He also prayed many other wonderful things, but as I examined his prayers I discovered he never asked for material things. He was more concerned with the spiritual than the material needs. His prayers were also filled with thanksgiving, which is a type of praise and worship. He said, for example, that every time he prayed, he thanked God for his partners in ministry. We should be thankful for the people God has given us, who help us in our lives and ministries.

I am sure Paul presented his physical needs to the Lord, but it is obvious that type of praying didn't fill up much of his prayer time. We see the same thing from Jesus' prayers. He didn't spend His time praying for material wants and needs; He knelt in the Garden and prayed to be strengthened to do the will of God. When He was weary from ministering to the people, He went into the mountains to pray, and I feel sure He was praising, not petitioning, God.

MAGNIFY THE LORD

O magnify the Lord with me, and let us exalt His name together.

PSALM 34:3

I will praise the name of God with a song and will magnify Him with thanksgiving.

PSALM 69:30

The word *magnify* means "to enlarge." When we tell God, "I magnify You," we are literally saying, "I make You bigger in my life than any problem or need that I have." I have sung many songs over the years that talked about magnifying the Lord without even realizing what the word meant. We do this a lot. We sing and talk about things we don't even really understand. They are just phrases we have learned in church.

We should magnify the Lord, and that means we should make Him larger than anything else in our life. When we worship and praise Him, we are doing just that. We are saying, "You are so big, so great, that I want to worship You." By putting worship first, we are also saying, "You're bigger than any need I have."

THE POWER OF WORSHIP

For it is written, As I live, says the Lord, every knee shall bow to Me, and every tongue shall confess to God [acknowledge Him to His honor and to His praise].

ROMANS 14:11

I believe that when we worship God, at least part of the time we need to assume a posture of worship. We need to bend the knee and bow down before Him. It is a sign of reverence and humility. It is an outward sign that states our heart attitude. Satan cannot see what is in our hearts, but he can see the knee bent in worship to God.

In Philippians 2:10,11 we are told, **That in (at) the name of Jesus every knee should (must) bow, in heaven and on earth . . . And every tongue [frankly and openly] confess and acknowledge that Jesus Christ is Lord, to the glory of God the Father. And in 1 Timothy 2:8, the apostle Paul tells us, I desire therefore that in every place men should pray, without anger or quarreling or resentment or doubt [in their minds], lifting up holy hands.**

Uplifted hands are another outward sign of worship. Why should we make all these outward signs? Isn't what's in our heart sufficient? As I have already said, the devil cannot see what is in our heart, but he certainly can see our actions and hear our words. When he can see by our posture and words that we are worshiping God, the devil starts getting afraid. He knows he cannot deceive and control a worshiper.

Satan can see the outward manifestation of our uplifted hands, and he knows what is going on when we bow down. Now, obviously, these are outward forms of worship, and we know that outward forms without a right heart attitude are useless. What we need to see is that both work together. Our heart attitude establishes things in the spiritual realm, and our actions and words establish them in this natural realm.

That is the reason why the Bible says that to be saved, we must believe with our heart and confess with our mouth that Jesus died and rose from the dead.

> *Because if you acknowledge and confess with your lips that Jesus is Lord and in your heart believe (adhere to, trust in, and rely on the truth) that God raised Him from the dead, you will be saved.*
>
> *For with the heart a person believes (adheres to, trusts in, and relies on Christ) and so is justified (declared righteous, acceptable to God), and with the mouth he confesses (declares openly and speaks out freely his faith) and confirms [his] salvation.*
>
> ROMANS 10:9,10

This is a very important principle that we are in danger of missing. We are saved by faith, but James said that faith without works is dead. I can believe in my heart that God is worthy of worship, but if I don't take action to worship Him, it doesn't do much good. I can say I believe in tithing, but if I don't tithe, it won't help me financially.

Water baptism is another biblical example of the same principle. It is an outward sign of an inward decision to follow Christ. The Bible teaches that when we receive Christ as our personal Savior, we are born again. Water baptism does not establish a relationship between the person and God; that comes as a result of the new birth. *The Amplified Bible* says that water baptism is a demonstration of what we believe to be ours through the resurrection of Jesus Christ.

Be bold — take some action and be expressive in your praise and worship. A lot of people even refuse to talk about God. They say, "Religion is a private thing." I cannot find anyone in the Bible who met Jesus and kept it private. When He fills our hearts, the good news about Him comes out of our mouths. When we are excited about praising and worshiping Him, it is difficult to have no outward expression. People who sit in church with sour, somber faces, never moving or expressing any joy, should do a thorough study on worship and praise and see how David and others in the Bible worshiped God.

Worship is not only something due God, but it is a powerful force that shakes heaven, earth and hell. Not only does the devil see the knee bent in true worship, but heaven does also. A worshiper gets God's attention. Heaven is filled with worship and praise.

> *The twenty-four elders (the members of the heavenly Sanhedrin) fall prostrate before Him Who is sitting on the throne, and they worship Him Who lives forever and ever. . . .*
>
> REVELATION 4:10

The scene in heaven this Scripture describes is actually repeated several times in the book of Revelation. We pray regularly . . . **Thy will be done in earth, as it is in heaven.** Therefore, we should apply heavenly principles to our worship while we are here on earth.

Become a dangerous Christian — become Christlike, let your praise outweigh your petition; trade worry for worship and be aggressive in your expression of how you feel about the Lord.

Chapter

8

Worship and Prayer

While He was talking this way to them, behold, a ruler entered and, kneeling down, worshiped Him, saying, My daughter has just now died; but come and lay Your hand on her, and she will come to life.

MATTHEW 9:18

T hat is exactly what happened. Jesus went and touched the girl, and she came back to life.

But notice the first thing this ruler did — not the last thing he did, but the first. He did not wait until he had a manifestation of his miracle and then bow down and worship Jesus. He worshiped Him before he ever asked Him to do anything for his daughter.

How many times have we asked God to change our friends or the people in our family without taking the time to worship Him first? "God, You've got to change my family. I just can't stand it any longer if You don't. You have got to change them, and that's all there is to it."

What would happen if, instead of doing that, we just bowed down and worshiped God, giving Him honor, thanks and praise? What if we even went a step further and put our face right to the ground like Elijah did on Mount Carmel or like Jehoshaphat did while waiting for God to give him victory over his enemies? We need to say things like, "Oh, God, I worship You. I magnify Your name, Lord. You are worthy to be praised. You strengthen me when I am weak. You enable me to do what I could never do without You. I know, O God, that You have my best interest in Your heart. You are good, Father, and I believe that Your goodness is surely going to manifest in my life. I believe that right now You are working in my life and in my circumstances. I believe that You are changing me and my family and friends. I believe that You are dealing with the ones who are not born again. I believe that they will accept You, be filled with Your Holy Spirit and manifest Your character in their life. I worship You, God, for the work You are doing right now and for Your faithfulness."

What do you believe would start happening? I believe we would start seeing changes in our life and circumstances, as well as changes in the people we love that need to take place. Change comes after we worship God, not before!

WORSHIP AND FAITH

And behold, a woman who was a Canaanite from that district came out and, with a [loud, troublesomely urgent] cry, begged, Have mercy on me, O Lord, Son of David! My daughter is miserably and distressingly and cruelly possessed by a demon!

But He did not answer her a word. And His disciples came and implored Him, saying, Send her away, for she is crying out after us.

MATTHEW 15:22,23

I think the reason that Jesus did not answer this woman was that she had not worshiped yet. She had just started following after Him, telling Him what she needed first.

He answered, I was sent only to the lost sheep of the house of Israel.

MATTHEW 15:24

Instead of helping her, He began to confront the woman's faith.

But she came and, kneeling, worshiped Him and kept praying, Lord, help me!

And He answered, It is not right (proper, becoming, or fair) to take the children's bread and throw it to the little dogs.

MATTHEW 15:25,26

Then, once she had begun worshiping Him, He went from confronting her faith to challenging her faith, but still she would not be denied.

She said, Yes, Lord, yet even the little pups (little whelps) eat the crumbs that fall from their [young] masters' table.

Then Jesus answered her, O woman, great is your faith! Be it done for you as you wish. And her daughter was cured from that moment.

MATTHEW 15:27,28

This woman's miracle did not come until two things had been established: 1) that she had faith, and 2) that she was going to worship God.

MORE THAN A METHOD

I am not trying to come up with a new set of rules and regulations for answered prayer. As I have mentioned previously, God sees our heart, and sincerity of heart is the most important thing to Him. Worshiping God first before making petitions is not a formula or method that will work like some magic charm to help us get what we want or need. Unless our worship is real and comes out of a heart of genuine thanksgiving and praise, we may as well forget about having any good results. Just because we get up in the morning and fall on our knees in praise and worship does not mean that everything in our life is going to change the way we want it to.

Just because we bow down or lift up our hands, that does not mean we are going to get whatever we ask for in prayer.

This is not just another method or formula to follow to get what we want out of God. If it is taken and applied that way, there will be no power in it.

A right heart attitude — one that is sincere and genuinely loves God and wants His will — is the basis for power. After that, the method can be used for the power to flow through. God is always, first and foremost, concerned with the motive of our heart. He always sees "the why behind the what." In other words, God is not just concerned with *what* we do, but His concern is *why* we are doing it.

If we are worshiping God inwardly and outwardly because we truly believe He is worthy of praise and worship, and we believe He is the only One Who can solve our problems and meet our needs, then and only then will we see positive results and see more answers to our prayers.

The Necessity of True Worship

A time will come, however, indeed it is already here, when the true (genuine) worshipers will worship the Father in spirit and in truth (reality); for the Father is seeking just such people as these as His worshipers.

God is a Spirit (a spiritual Being) and those who worship Him must worship Him in spirit and in truth (reality).

JOHN 4:23,24

Sometimes we can walk into a church service and sense a strong spirit of worship among the people. We can sense they are caught up in God's Presence and are truly worshiping Him in truth (or reality). But there may be some people there who are just mouthing the words and not really entering wholeheartedly into the praise and worship. We should not honor Him with our lips while our hearts are far from Him.

A man once told about a vision he had. He was in a church service one day while the people were involved in praise and deep worship. In that atmosphere, God spoke to him and said, "I am going to show you the people in here who are really worshiping Me. There is a light coming off of each one of them."

The man said that out of that whole congregation, there were only about three or four who had the light coming from them. The rest of the people in that congregation were just going through the motions of worshiping, while their mind was on something else.

When we worship at home alone, we are probably less likely to get distracted, although even then our minds have a tendency to wander off to other things. We must discipline ourselves to fix our minds on the Lord when worshiping Him.

I strongly urge people to be on time for church so they don't interrupt others who are trying to enter into praise and worship as they attempt to find seats. If we cannot be on time, we should probably wait in the back of the church until praise and worship has ended, just to show reverence and respect to God and other people. I have even been to some churches where the doors were closed when praise and worship began, and the crowd that came late could not enter until it was over. They could hear the praise and worship through loud speakers as they waited in the vestibule, but in order not to disturb others, they had to wait to find seats. Some people may find this too rigid, but it might also encourage people to be on time.

The other option is to find an empty seat in the back of the auditorium, where others will not be disturbed or distracted by our entrance.

We are all late on occasion for reasons beyond our control, but some people are habitually late. No matter what time the service began they would be late.

It is too bad we are so easily distracted. Satan can easily use this weakness in us to prevent us from ever entering into high praise or deep worship. Notice I used the words "high" and "deep." There is a big difference in singing songs and truly getting lost in the Presence of God. We want to praise and worship God with all of our hearts.

I often stop the praise in our conferences and exhort the people to really pay attention to the words they are singing. I can tell that many of them are just repeating words while they glance around the congregation, watching all the people as they try to get settled. I don't like that, and I know the praise and worship won't help them much or honor God if they don't concentrate on what they are doing. After I give this exhortation, I can always tell a big difference in the spiritual atmosphere. People are making an effort not to become distracted. The result is that a stronger anointing, or Presence of the Holy Spirit, invades the room.

To summarize, the first thing we need to do is make sure our heart attitude is right. Then we should be expressive so the devil can plainly see we are worshiping.

ACTIONS AS DECLARATIONS

For every time you eat this bread and drink this cup, you are representing and signifying and proclaiming the fact of the Lord's death until He comes [again].

1 CORINTHIANS 11:26

I personally believe that Communion is another way that we express outwardly what is happening inwardly. The Bible says that every time we eat the bread and drink the cup, we are remembering Christ's body and His blood and proclaiming His death until He comes back.

We need to understand that when we take Communion, we are making a declaration of faith with our actions and not just with what we say we believe in our heart.

People often say, "My heart is right," but people cannot read our heart; they can only see our actions. That is just as foolish as a man telling his wife, "You should know I love you; I married you didn't I?" yet he never shows her any affection or gives her any reason in her emotions or mind to believe him. *It is important that we show, with our actions, what we believe in our heart.*

When I take Communion, I always say, "Lord Jesus, as I take this bread, I am taking You as my Living Bread. As long as I eat of You and fellowship with You, I will never be dissatisfied. As I take this drink, I am drinking Living Water. As long as I drink of You and fellowship with You, I will be satisfied to the point where I am not disturbed, no matter what my outward circumstances may be. I am declaring by the taking of this Communion, Lord Jesus, that You are all I need in life to be truly happy and fulfilled."

Then I go on to say: "There are many other things that I would love to have and enjoy. I can live without them if I have to, but I cannot live without You. You are my number-one need."

When we start acting like that, the devil starts getting nervous. Satan knows that if we get into that kind of close relationship with the Lord, he can no longer control us.

DECLARE IT WITH ACTIONS!

O clap your hands, all you peoples! Shout to God with the voice of triumph and songs of joy!

PSALM 47:1

The Bible instructs us to dance, to play musical instruments and to do all kinds of outward things to express worship to the Lord. We need it; it brings a release in our life, it honors God and it aids in defeating the devil.

It is not enough just to say, "Well, God knows how I feel about Him. I don't have to make a big display." That would be no different from saying, "Well, God knows I believe in Him; therefore, there is no real need for me to be baptized." Or to say,

"God knows I am sorry for my sins; therefore, there is no need for me to admit my sins and repent of them." We readily see how foolish this would be, and people from all denominations would agree that we need to be baptized and confess our sins. Yet all denominations don't teach people to have outward expression of their praise and worship.

I attended a church for many years, which is known all around the world. We sang songs from a hymnal as a part of each service, but there was no outward expression of clapping, dancing or uplifted hands. As a matter of fact, one would have felt they were doing something wrong if they did those things. The Bible talks about all of these things, and yet this church, as well as many others, felt that reverence was the only proper display of our worship. We definitely need times of being quiet and reverent, but we also need the release of emotions in worship.

I am not encouraging unbridled emotion. We all know there are people who just get "emotional," and they can actually become a distraction. What we need is balance. Just because some individuals have been overly emotional in the past, some denominations entirely rule out showing any emotion in church. I personally believe that if we had a proper emotional release during praise and worship, we might not release emotions at other times in an improper way. Our emotions are just as much a part of us as our body, mind, will or spirit. God gave us emotions, and they must be cared for like the rest of us. We are not to be controlled by emotions because they are known to be fickle or untrustworthy, but neither can we stifle them and be whole.

As I sat in the church I mentioned above, there were times when emotions would well up inside me. I felt a need to express them in some way but had no idea how to do so. I think it is tragic not to teach people that they are free to express themselves and their love for God in a balanced way. It is wrong to be so afraid of something getting out of balance that we cut it off altogether.

Each of us can say of our particular denomination, "Well, that is just the way we do things." I don't feel that is a proper attitude. We all must be open to growth, which always means change. Jesus said that He could not pour new wine into old wineskins, meaning some of the old ways had to go. They had to "let go" of old things and take hold of the new. Knowledge and revelation is progressive; if a thing isn't moving, it is at the point of dying.

It is not my intention to sound judgmental; however, the Word of God is our guideline of accuracy. The things I am sharing are all backed up by Scripture, which we should all be willing to submit to.

I encourage you to begin being expressive in your praise and worship at home if you attend a church where it would be unacceptable to do so in the public service. I also encourage you to pray for positive change so everyone can be taught to worship God as He truly deserves to be worshiped.

Declare It with Words

Through Him, therefore, let us constantly and at all times offer up to God a sacrifice of praise, which is the fruit of lips that thankfully acknowledge and confess and glorify His name.

HEBREWS 13:15

The confession of our mouth is a powerful weapon against the enemy. Proverbs 18:21 teaches us that the power of life and death is in the tongue. We can speak life to ourselves and death to Satan's plan of destruction. Words of thanksgiving, for example, are devastating to the devil. He absolutely hates to hear a thankful person talking about the goodness of God.

Hebrews 4:12 teaches us that the Word of God is a sharp two-edged sword. I believe that one edge of the sword defeats Satan, while the other edge slices open the blessings of heaven. We are told in Ephesians 6:17 that the sword the Spirit wields, which is the Word of God, is one of our pieces of armor to be worn in order to effectively do spiritual warfare.

David the psalmist frequently made statements like, **I will say of the Lord, He is my Refuge and my Fortress, my God; on Him I lean and rely, and in Him I [confidently] trust!** Perhaps we should regularly ask ourselves, "What am I saying of the Lord?" We need to SAY right things, not just think them. A person may think, "I believe all those good things about the Lord," but are you *saying* anything that is helping you? Often people claim to believe something, yet the opposite comes out of their mouth.

We need to talk out loud. We need to do it at proper times and in proper places, but we need to be sure we do it. Let verbal confessions become part of your fellowship time with God. I often take walks in the morning. I pray, I sing and I confess the Word out loud. Each time I say something like, "God is on my side. I can do whatever He assigns me to do." Or "God is good, and He has a good plan for my life. Blessings are chasing me and overflowing in my life." It is equivalent to me jabbing Satan with a sharp sword.

Verbalize your thanksgiving, your praise and your worship. Sing songs out loud that are filled with praise and worship. Take some aggressive action against the enemy!

THE POWER OF UPLIFTED HANDS

O God, You are my God, earnestly will I seek You; my inner self thirsts for You, my flesh longs and is faint for You, in a dry and weary land where no water is.

So I have looked upon You in the sanctuary to see Your power and Your glory.

Because Your loving-kindness is better than life, my lips shall praise You.

So will I bless You while I live; I will lift up my hands in Your name.

PSALM 63:1-4

Sacrifice and Christianity have always been connected. In the Old Testament, the law required sacrifices of various kinds. David speaks of lifting up the **hands as the evening sacrifice** in Psalm 141:2.

There are several other Scripture references concerning the lifting up of hands. It seems a natural thing to do when we are in the Presence of God. To me, it is an expression of adoration, reverence and surrender. We should continually surrender ourselves to God and His plan for us.

You can lift your hands up and speak a word of praise all throughout the day. Even at work, you can go to the bathroom and take a moment to praise God. When we surrender, God takes control. He is a gentleman and will not force His will on us. He waits for us to let Him know that we have placed our trust in Him. I encourage you to begin lifting up your hands and offering words of praise. Not only will it bless the Lord, but also it will help to defeat the devil, and you will feel better.

People who have never in their entire life lifted up their hands in praise and worship to God may have a mighty release of pent-up emotions. Our spirit longs to worship aggressively and expressively; there is something missing for us spiritually until we do it. I was a Christian for many years before I ever did this. I was longing for a release in praise and worship, but I didn't even have enough teaching to know what I needed.

TAKE A PRAISE PAUSE

Seven times a day and all day long do I praise You because of Your righteous decrees.

PSALM 119:164

I don't think anything blesses God more than when we stop right in the middle of what we're doing sometimes and lift our hands to worship Him, or take a moment to bow down before Him and say, "I love You, Lord." In the Scripture quoted above, the psalmist says he took time seven times a day and all day long to praise God.

Think about a businessman, for example, maybe the president of a large company. Wouldn't it be wonderful if two or three times a day, he would close the door to his office, turn the lock, kneel and say, "God, I just want to take some time to worship You. Father, all these things You are giving me — the business, the money, the success — are great, but I just want to worship

You. I magnify You. You are so wonderful. I love You. You are all I need. Father, I worship You. Jesus, I worship You. Holy Spirit, I worship You."

I believe that if that businessman did that, he would never need to be concerned about his business, his finances or success. All of those things would be taken care of.

> *But seek ye first the kingdom of God, and his righteousness; and all these things shall be added unto you.*
>
> MATTHEW 6:33 KJV

A housewife would have many more fruitful, peaceful days if she took time to do this. There is no person who would not benefit greatly from taking a "praise pause."

As well as taking a praise pause, just to honor God, we should do as I have mentioned anytime we feel stressed out, extremely tired, frustrated or like giving up. It will refresh us. Taking this type of action is, once again, expressing our total dependence upon the Lord. We must remember that He said, . . . **apart from me you can do nothing** (John 15:5 NIV).

WHY BOW DOWN?

> *Now when Daniel knew that the writing was signed, he went into his house, and his windows being open in his chamber toward Jerusalem, he got down upon his knees three times a day and prayed and gave thanks before his God, as he had done previously.*
>
> DANIEL 6:10

Why should we bow down? When we do so, we are humbling ourselves. We are saying by our actions, "Lord, I reverence

You and honor You. You are everything, and I am nothing without You. I can do nothing without You, and do it properly. If You don't help me, I am lost because there is no one else who can really help me except You."

Do you remember the story of Daniel and the lions' den? Daniel's enemies were jealous of him and his high position in the kingdom. Because Daniel was a righteous man, they knew there was no way to bring an accusation against him because of any wrong behavior. They sought to find a way to flaw his devotion to God through fear of harm. They persuaded the king to issue a decree that for thirty days anyone caught petitioning any god or man except the king would be thrown into the lions' den.

Daniel's enemies knew that it was his habit to go into his room three times a day, open the windows toward Jerusalem and kneel down and pray and worship God.

Daniel refused to compromise on his worship. The next time he worshiped God in this way, his enemies caught him and brought him before the king, who had no choice but to have him thrown into the lions' den. I love the part of this story that says he prayed with his windows open, as was his custom. In other words, he was not trying to keep it a secret. He had reverential fear and awe for God that was greater than any fear of man.

Daniel did have to go into the lions' den but slept that night and came out the next day unharmed because God had shut the mouths of the lions. Instead of him being devoured by the lions, his enemies were thrown into the lions' den and destroyed.

If you and I will worship God when our enemies conspire to bring harm to us, like Daniel we will come out unharmed.

Bow Down to Be Raised Up

They came to the other side of the sea to the region of the Gerasenes.

And as soon as He got out of the boat, there met Him out of the tombs a man [under the power] of an unclean spirit.

This man continually lived among the tombs, and no one could subdue him any more, even with a chain;

For he had been bound often with shackles for the feet and handcuffs, but the handcuffs of [light] chains he wrenched apart, and the shackles he rubbed and ground together and broke in pieces; and no one had strength enough to restrain or tame him

Night and day among the tombs and on the mountains he was always shrieking and screaming and beating and bruising and cutting himself with stones.

And when from a distance he saw Jesus, he ran and fell on his knees before Him in homage.

MARK 5:1-6

You may think you have problems, but they are nothing compared to the problems this poor man had. But notice what he did as soon as he saw Jesus — he ran and fell on his knees and worshiped Him. The rest of the story is that Jesus cast a legion of demons out of the man, and he went on his way completely free.

No matter how many problems you may have, if you will begin to fall on your knees or bow your face to the ground on a regular basis in worship and adoration of God, I can promise you that He will bring you through to a place of victory.

We don't just want to worship God when something wonderful has happened, and we are excited and feel like worshiping.

These are good times to worship, but we also especially need to worship in hard times.

The Lord once told me that the reason most people stay desperate much of the time is because that is the only time they will seek Him. He said to me, "Joyce, if you will seek Me as if you're desperate all the time, you won't have as many desperate times in your life."

The Israelites spent many years in the wilderness where God was trying to teach them to do things right. As I already mentioned, they spent forty years trying to make an eleven-day journey. They repeatedly sought God when they were desperate and forgot all about Him when times were good. God would allow their enemies to be in control because they were not seeking Him, and then they would seek Him again. Things were good when they sought God and bad when they didn't. In Deuteronomy 8:2 we read, **And you shall [earnestly] remember all the way which the Lord your God led you these forty years in the wilderness, to humble you and to prove you, to know what was in your [mind and] heart, whether you would keep His commandments or not.**

A part of His commandments was for them to worship Him at all times, yet many of them never learned the lesson; therefore, they didn't enter the Promised Land. Actually, only two of the original possibly one and one half million people who left Egypt actually entered the Promised Land. This is extremely sad and actually shocking. We might think, "How could that be?" Yet, in reality, how many people do you know who truly live in victory regularly? Victory is not the absence of problems; it is having peace and joy in the midst of them. Victory is continuing to bear good fruit for the kingdom of God, even when we are going through difficulty personally.

> *Thus says the Lord: Cursed [with great evil] is the strong man who trusts in and relies on frail man, making weak [human] flesh his arm, and whose mind and heart turn aside from the Lord.*
>
> *For he shall be like a shrub or a person naked and destitute in the desert; and he shall not see any good come, but shall dwell in the parched places in the wilderness, in an uninhabited salt land.*
>
> *[Most] blessed is the man who believes in, trusts in, and relies on the Lord, and whose hope and confidence the Lord is.*
>
> *For he shall be like a tree planted by the waters that spreads out its roots by the river; and it shall not see and fear when heat comes; but its leaf shall be green. It shall not be anxious and full of care in the year of drought, nor shall it cease yielding fruit.*
>
> JEREMIAH 17:5-8

These Scriptures say that the person who regularly seeks God and does not lean on man to solve his problems will be very stable. In a whole year of drought, that person shall continue to bear good fruit. I believe that this is one of the most important things we need to do in order to be a good witness. If Satan can control our behavior with his attacks, they will never stop. But, on the other hand, if we remain in the state God desires us to be in, no matter what the enemy brings against us, we show by our behavior that our faith in God is working to produce not only right behavior, but peace and joy. Our lives will become salt and light; others will want what we have, and they will be open to us sharing our faith with them.

When we regularly put God first, when we worship Him and take time to bow before Him, He will always lift us up.

Worship and Change

While he was still speaking, behold a shining cloud [composed of light] overshadowed them, and a voice from the cloud said, This is My Son, My Beloved, with Whom I am [and have always been] delighted. Listen to Him!

MATTHEW 17:5

In an earlier chapter, we read how Jesus took three of His disciples and went up on a mountain to pray and how as He was worshiping God, He was transfigured before their very eyes. Here in this verse, we see what God said to the disciples about Jesus at that moment: **This is My beloved Son, in whom I am well pleased** (NKJV).

I believe that every person who wants to be powerful in God needs to hear God speak that same message to him or her. As God's own dearly beloved children, each one of us needs to know that God is pleased w ith us personally and individually.

It is my desire and my prayer that by the time you have finished reading this book, you will know that God is pleased with you.

I write that knowing that you are probably already rejecting it: "Oh, no, God can't be pleased with me, not the way I act."

God is not pleased with you because you do everything right. He is pleased with you because you put your faith in Jesus, the One Who did everything right for you.

WHAT JESUS DID FOR US

For our sake He made Christ [virtually] to be sin Who knew no sin, so that in and through Him we might become [endued with, viewed as being in, and examples of] the righteousness of God [what we ought to be, approved and acceptable and in right relationship with Him, by His goodness].

2 CORINTHIANS 5:21

I don't think most of us truly understand the concept of Jesus being our Substitute. This means that He took our place and suffered all that we deserve so that we could take His place and enjoy all that He deserves.

Take the example of a schoolteacher. If she must miss a day of school, a substitute is called in to take her place for that day. If the substitute is qualified and does what she is assigned to do, the regular teacher does not have to go back and redo the work that was done while she was out — it was done for her by her substitute.

Jesus was our Substitute. Because of what He has done for us, we have been made **heirs of God, and joint-heirs with Christ** (Romans 8:17 KJV). The Bible says that we have been made more than conquerors and have gained a surpassing victory through Him Who loved us and gave Himself for us. (Romans 8:37.)

Do you know what it means for each of us to be more than a conqueror? It means that Jesus conquered, and we get the victory.

Do you know what it means to be heirs of God and joint-heirs with Christ? It means that Jesus did whatever was required in relationship to become the Heir and Possessor of everything that God, the Father, has — and then He turned to us and said, "Now, if you put faith in Me, you are a joint-heir with Me." Because of faith, we obtain everything Jesus earned and deserves.

If I inherited some money, my children would automatically become joint-heirs with me in my inheritance. That is exactly what has happened to us; Jesus has been made Heir of everything the Father possesses, and by taking our place, He has made us joint-heirs of it all with Him.

If we truly understand what has been done for us through the substitutionary work of Jesus Christ, we will start living in the fullness of joy and peace that God has always intended for us. We will be so happy about being saved — if we really understand what it means to be saved.

THE MEANING OF SALVATION

In Luke 10:20 Jesus told His disciples, "Don't rejoice that demons are subject to you in My name, but rejoice that your names are written in heaven."

I believe our level of joy as believers in Jesus Christ is directly connected to our depth of knowledge concerning what it means to be saved. It means that because we have placed our faith in God's Son Jesus Christ, we are saved from hell, damnation, sin, guilt and condemnation. But it also means that because the nature of Almighty God has been deposited on the inside of us, and because we have in our spirit the incorruptible seed of Almighty God, we can be assured that we are going to change.

> *No one born (begotten) of God [deliberately, knowingly, and habit-ually] practices sin, for God's nature abides in him [His principle of life, the divine sperm, remains permanently within him]; and he cannot practice sinning because he is born (begotten) of God.*
>
> 1 JOHN 3:9

The Bible says that because of what Jesus Christ accomplished on the cross for us, death has been swallowed up in life. Whatever there is in our flesh that partakes of death is not strong enough to withstand God inside of us producing life.

Because you and I have the life of God within us, we are changing from day to day, and there is nothing the enemy can do about it. God is working in us, completing what He began.

When the devil begins to accuse us and tries to make us feel bad about ourselves, we should tell him, "Satan, you are a liar. I'm growing spiritually every day. I'm getting sweeter and sweeter. I'm loving people more and more. I'm becoming more caring and more generous. I'm giving away things quicker when God tells me to do so. I'm becoming more joyful, more kind and compassionate, more gentle and peaceful every day that goes by — and there is nothing you can do about it, devil. God is in me; He is changing me! You can tell me how rotten I am, and I will tell you who I am in Christ."

Right in the midst of all the devil's accusations we should say, "Thank You, Lord, that You are changing me. I worship You.

I magnify Your name. There is none like You. I love You, Lord. I love You; I love You; I love You."

The Power of Private Praise

But when you pray, go into your [most] private room, and, closing the door, pray to your Father, Who is in secret; and your Father, Who sees in secret, will reward you in the open.

MATTHEW 6:6

I sincerely believe that if you will begin to bow down and worship God the way King David did, you will begin to see some marvelous things take place in your life. You will experience release from bondage.

As Jesus has told us, there are some things we are to do in private. There are times when I go into my bedroom, lock the door and dance and worship before the Lord, sometimes crying and sometimes laughing all by myself. If anybody saw me, they might think I needed to be locked up. In private, I express myself freely with no inhibitions; I don't need to be concerned about offending or confusing anyone.

If you do these things openly, the world will tell you that you are crazy. They do not understand how you feel because they don't have the relationship with God that you have. However, you can do them in private, between you and God alone, and you will see good fruit develop in your life. The fruit comes from what God sees, not what people see.

I believe that all of us ought to get in a private place and rejoice before the Lord, bow down before Him, lift up our hands

THE BATTLE BELONGS TO THE LORD

to Him in praise, and if we need to, even weep in His Presence. Worship and praise should not be confined to the church service.

I worship God publicly when I gather with other people who are worshiping, and I worship at home alone. Both private and public praise and worship are very important. I encourage you to frequently enter into both.

What Must I Do to Please God?

They then said, What are we to do, that we may [habitually] be working the works of God? [What are we to do to carry out what God requires?]

Jesus replied, This is the work (service) that God asks of you: that you believe in the One Whom He has sent [that you cleave to, trust, rely on, and have faith in His Messenger].

JOHN 6:28,29

God is changing me, and He is changing you. And He is pleased with us. We are not where we need to be, but thank God, we are not where we used to be. The Lord looks at our progress, not just how far we have to go.

In John chapter 6 some people asked Jesus, "What are we supposed to do to work the works of God?" What they were really asking Him was, "What must we do to please God?"

Jesus answered them by saying, "Believe."

What Jesus was telling them when He said to believe was that they were to believe what the Scriptures said about Him.

What do the Scriptures say to us about Jesus? They tell us that He Who knew no sin became sin for us that we might be made the righteousness of God in Him. (2 Corinthians 5:21.) As we have seen, the Scriptures also tell us that He is changing us, and we are experiencing higher degrees of glory. (2 Corinthians 3:18.) Little by little our enemies are defeated. (Deuteronomy 7:22.) Change is a process that takes time.

If all this is true, then why do we have such a hard time believing that daily we are being changed, that through the power of the indwelling Holy Spirit, we are being transformed and transfigured? We must believe before we see — that is the way things work in God's economy. In the world we are taught to believe what we see, but God is teaching us to believe what He says, and then we will see.

In our carnality we ask, "What shall we do?" We must learn that the work assigned to us is spiritual — we are to believe. We are "believers," not "achievers." We believe, and the Holy Spirit works in us.

We are to enter God's rest and believe that He is working in our behalf. (Hebrews 4:3,10,11.) He is seated in heavenly places, and we are seated in Him. (Ephesians 2:6.) To be seated signifies rest. Jesus is waiting for Father God to make all of His enemies a footstool for His feet. (Hebrews 1:13.) We are waiting for the same thing in our own lives. Each day we are closer to complete victory. Hallelujah!

When we praise God before we see change, we are saying with our actions that we believe. We have entered His rest; we are seated and waiting for Him to make our enemies a footstool for our feet. As we praise God during our times of waiting, we are declaring that we believe we already have the victory, and we are simply waiting for it to manifest. We are giving evidence that we believe the battle belongs to the Lord.

Chapter
10

Worship God with a Pure Conscience

I thank God Whom I worship with a pure conscience, in the spirit of my fathers, when without ceasing I remember you night and day in my prayers.

2 Timothy 1:3

True worship must come from the heart of the worshiper. It is not, and can never be, merely a learned behavior. God is interested in the heart of man above all else. If the heart is not pure, nothing that comes from the man is acceptable to God.

Any works offered with impure motives are unacceptable and so is feigned worship that does not come from a pure heart and a clean conscience.

The conscience is actually man's best friend in that it continually and unrelentingly helps the believer know what is pleasing to God and what is not pleasing. It is the best preacher anyone can ever have in their life and is designed to teach us God's will.

The conscience is enlightened by God's Word; therefore, the more of His Word one learns the more active the conscience will be. There are things I am convicted of as being wrong now in my life that even a few years ago I felt very little or no conviction about. Although I have been a Christian since I was nine years old, I only became a really serious, committed Christian in 1976. I suppose I was growing spiritually all the time previous to 1976, but it was minor growth compared to what I have experienced since then.

The main reason for the change is that I really began to study God's Word in 1976 after the Holy Spirit filled my life in a new way. Although I was born again previous to that time, I was not filled with the Holy Spirit. I had the Holy Spirit in my life, but I usually say, "The Holy Spirit did not have me."

I compromised a lot. I had one foot in the kingdom of God and the other one in the world. I was a lukewarm believer. I had enough of Jesus to keep me out of hell but not enough to cause me to walk in victory. Obviously, Jesus does not come in pieces so, in reality, I had all of Him, but He did not have all of me. Therefore, I was carnal and not a good witness for the cause of Christ.

AN ENLIGHTENED CONSCIENCE

I am speaking the truth in Christ. I am not lying; my conscience [enlightened and prompted] by the Holy Spirit bearing witness with me.

ROMANS 9:1

We see that Paul referred to his conscience being enlightened by the Holy Spirit. Paul could tell by his conscience that his behavior was acceptable to God, and I am sure that he could, likewise, discern when it was not. That is the function of the conscience.

Paul spoke of the importance of keeping one's conscience clean. One of the main functions of the Holy Spirit in our lives is to teach us all truth, to convict us of sin and convince us of righteousness. (John 16:8,13.)

> *Therefore I always exercise and discipline myself [mortifying my body, deadening my carnal affections, bodily appetites, and worldly desires, endeavoring in all respects] to have a clear (unshaken, blameless) conscience, void of offense toward God and toward men.*

> ACTS 24:16

Since Paul made such an effort to have a clear conscience, it surely must be very important. As we saw from 2 Timothy 1:3, Paul worshiped God with a clear, clean conscience. That is also the only way we can offer acceptable worship.

It is important to me that I bring this point out clearly. I do not want to offer methods called "worship" as a means of obtaining victory or blessings from the Lord. He definitely does bring victory into the life of the worshiper, but as I said previously, one is not truly a worshiper unless the worship is offered from a pure heart and a clean conscience.

Simply stated that means we cannot properly worship God with known sin in our lives. The confession of sin should be the prelude to real worship. We must approach God with a clean conscience. There is no peace for the person with a guilty conscience. His faith will not work; therefore, his prayers won't be answered. The two Scriptures that follow bear this out.

> *Holding fast to faith (that leaning of the entire human personality on God in absolute trust and confidence) and having a good (clear)*

conscience. By rejecting and thrusting from them [their conscience], some individuals have made shipwreck of their faith.

1 TIMOTHY 1:19

They must possess the mystic secret of the faith [Christian truth as hidden from ungodly men] with a clear conscience.

1 TIMOTHY 3:9

BE PERFECT

You, therefore, must be perfect [growing into complete maturity of godliness in mind and character, having reached the proper height of virtue and integrity], as your heavenly Father is perfect.

MATTHEW 5:48

The Bible commands us to be perfect even as our Father in heaven is perfect. Unless we understand that properly, we immediately feel defeated and even fearful. *The Amplified Bible* translation quoted above makes it clear. "Perfect" is a state of spiritual maturity that we grow into. We must continue pressing toward the mark of perfection out of a sincere heart of wanting to please God, daily letting go of mistakes that lie behind.

In others words, our hearts can be perfect, but our behavior is not. We improve all the time and thank God for it, but we have not arrived. The Bible says that in the twinkling of an eye we shall all be changed. I believe that whatever remains to be done in each of us, when Jesus returns, it will be done in the twinkling of an eye. In the meantime, we keep growing and pressing toward the mark.

The Pathway to a Clear Conscience

To have a clear conscience, one must either not sin or confess his sins when he does err and make mistakes. We do grow and find that we sin less as time goes by; however, the Bible teaches us that a little leaven affects the entire lump of dough. Even a little sin renders us in need of cleansing.

It is great to be making progress daily, but I am very thankful for the gift of repentance. First John 1:9 states that we can admit our sins, confess them, and that God is faithful to completely cleanse us of all unrighteousness. What good news! We can live before God with a perfectly clear conscience.

Paul did not live before God and man with a perfectly clear conscience because he never made mistakes. We know the exact opposite is true. He did make mistakes. He called himself the chief of all sinners and said that he had not arrived at the place of perfection.

Through hearty obedience and using the gift of repentance when Paul failed, he lived before God and man with a clear conscience and was, therefore, enabled to worship God properly and release his faith to see his needs met.

Why do I refer to repentance as a gift? I have seen people who could not feel sorry for their sins, and it is a terrible thing. When the conscience is seared (hardened), man is unable to feel the weight and seriousness of his wrong behavior. Because of this we should all pray for a tender conscience toward God.

What to Do When Your Conscience Convicts You

Conviction is not meant to condemn; it is rather intended to provoke us to repentance. It is intended to help you and me feel better, not worse. For years I did not know this truth. Each time the Holy Spirit convicted me of sin, I immediately felt guilty and condemned. It was actually quite horrible for me. I had become a serious student of God's Word; therefore, the more I studied the more I was convicted of sin, so it seemed I was feeling guilty and condemned all the time.

It was a wonderful day of release for me when I finally saw the truth. The truth does set us free, as John 8:32 says. Now I am glad when I feel convicted of sin in my life. I am not glad I am sinning, but I am glad that I can now repent of the sin and ask God to help me grow beyond it. I can also discern now when Satan is just trying to make me feel guilty and when my conscience, enlightened by the Holy Spirit, is really convicting me.

You must be aware that Satan is a legalist and the accuser of the brethren. There is a difference between his false accusations and true godly conviction.

I really want to encourage you not to do things that you don't have peace about doing. Let your conscience be your friend, not a source of torment. Colossians 3:15 states that peace is the umpire in our life that should settle with finality all things that raise a question in our minds. In other words, if a thing feels peaceful, it is in, and if it does not feel peaceful, it should be thrown out.

Being tempted by sin is not the same as sinning. Temptation is not a sin. We are all tempted to do wrong; Satan makes sure of that. When we are tempted, though, we can call on the Holy Spirit to help us resist. Don't try to resist in your own strength and power; ask for the Holy Spirit's help. He is always standing by to help you with anything you need in life.

AN EXAMPLE FROM KING DAVID'S LIFE

Blessed (happy, fortunate, to be envied) is he who has forgiveness of his transgression continually exercised upon him, whose sin is covered.

Blessed (happy, fortunate, to be envied) is the man to whom the Lord imputes no iniquity and in whose spirit there is no deceit.

When I kept silence [before I confessed], my bones wasted away through my groaning all the day long.

For day and night Your hand [of displeasure] was heavy upon me; my moisture was turned into the drought of summer. Selah [pause, and calmly think of that]!

I acknowledged my sin to You, and my iniquity I did not hide. I said, I will confess my transgressions to the Lord [continually unfolding the past till all is told] — then You [instantly] forgave me the guilt and iniquity of my sin. Selah [pause, and calmly think of that]!

For this [forgiveness] let everyone who is godly pray — pray to You in time when You may be found; surely when the great waters [of trial] overflow, they shall not reach [the spirit in] him.

You are a hiding place for me; You, Lord, preserve me from trouble, You surround me with songs and shouts of deliverance. Selah [pause, and calmly think of that]!

PSALM 32:1-7

King David was quite miserable until he finally repented of his sin. The verses above clearly show that his joy returned only after he repented. David had committed adultery with Bathsheba and killed her husband. A year had gone by, and he was still ignoring the issue. He was probably doing what we are all tempted to do when we sin — he was making excuses and being deceived by his own reasoning. All of us may not deal with sins as serious as what David was facing, but sin is sin, and it has a similar affect on us no matter what type of sin it is. The point is, until we admit it, confess and repent (which is to turn entirely away from it and go in another direction), we will not be able to worship God out of a pure heart, or with a clean conscience.

Notice in verse 7 how David states that God has now surrounded him with songs of deliverance. After his confession of sin, he is singing and shouting. That sounds like praise and worship to me.

OBEDIENCE IS THE BEST

The amount of disobedience among people who consider themselves to be a Christian is absolutely shocking. As you are probably acutely aware, we are experiencing a severe moral decline in our society today. As Christians, we are in the world but are not supposed to be of the world, according to what Jesus said. The difference between the world and those who are believers in Jesus Christ can be simply stated. Those of the world run their own lives. They do whatever they want to do, or feel like doing, without regard for how it affects others, or whether or not it is approved of by God.

Christians, on the other hand, are supposed to seek to walk in the will of God. They are to be led, guided and willingly controlled by the Holy Spirit because He will always lead us into the will of God.

There are dozens of issues that come up every day that require a decision. Our conscience helps us make those decisions. The Word of God and the promptings of the Holy Spirit help us make those decisions. But the fact remains that *we* make the decisions. God wants us to choose His will, but He will not force it upon us.

Jesus said in John 14:15, **If you [really] love Me, you will keep (obey) My commands.** Please notice that He did not say, "If you keep My commands, I will love you." God's love for us is unconditional. He loves us because He is love, not because of something we do or don't do. However, we show our love for Him through our willingness to obey Him. Obedience often hurts.

Anytime we don't get our own way, or we choose to do something we really don't want to do, it hurts. When our feelings don't support us, it is more difficult to do a thing. We have feelings, but we also have a will. Your will is the big boss; it is the "organ" that decides with finality what will or won't be done. It is stronger than the mind and stronger than feelings. When we willfully choose to do what God has asked us to do, even though our thoughts and feelings are not supporting us, it shows our love for the Lord.

Obedience is in itself a type of worship. Anytime I am confronted with a difficult situation and I choose to go God's way instead of my own, I am worshiping and honoring God. I am showing reverential fear and awe and saying by my actions that I am placing God above myself or how I feel.

I believe that there are people who attempt to offer what they think is worship, but it is not the kind of worship that God desires because it is being offered with known disobedience or a guilty conscience. Remember that John 4:24 states that God is looking for worshipers who worship Him in spirit and in truth. Making excuses for sin, or being self-deceived, is not truth.

THANK GOD FOR FORGIVENESS

As I said, obedience is always the best. But as I have also said, we all make mistakes. There are times when even the most dedicated Christians make wrong choices. That's when we need to quickly repent and ask for and receive God's forgiveness. I am not making a law or a rule of it, but probably the best thing to do is always begin our prayers with repentance for sin. Just ask God to forgive you for anything you have done wrong. If you are aware of specific situations, mention them. If nothing particular comes to mind, then ask Him to forgive any sin in your life, even ones that you may not be seeing as of yet. Ask the Lord to convict you of sin, telling Him that you want to do things right. Ask Him for grace, which is His enabling power to help you do whatever it is that He shows you needs to be corrected.

After taking the action above, you and I should be able to worship with a clean conscience.

Chapter

11

Transformation and Transfiguration

===

Do not be conformed to this world (this age), [fashioned after and adapted to its external, superficial customs], but be transformed (changed). . . .

ROMANS 12:2

As we have seen, the Bible talks about transformation and transfiguration. If we study these words, we learn that they both come from the Greek word *metamorphoo*, meaning "to change into another form."[1]

We have a great example of this process of metamorphosis in tadpoles, which become frogs, and caterpillars, which become butterflies.

In preparing to write this section on metamorphosis, I studied the subject. A caterpillar changing into a butterfly is the best example of metamorphosis. A caterpillar eats until it grows to a certain size. At that time it surrounds itself with a covering, called a cocoon, which it spins. It may burrow into the ground or hide behind a piece of loose bark. You might say it is a type of burial.

I can relate to the thought of burial because the Bible teaches us that we must die to self in order to live wholly for Christ. The apostle Paul said in Galatians 2:20, **I have been crucified with Christ [in Him I have shared His crucifixion]; it is** no longer I who live, but Christ (the Messiah) lives in me; and the life I now live in the body I live by faith in (by adherence to and reliance on and complete trust in) the Son of God, Who loved me and gave Himself up for me.

I have experienced this dying to self, and still do, when God is dealing with me about something I want that is not His will for me. There are things we must die to: attitudes, thought patterns, ways of acting and speaking, our own plans and desires. It is much easier to discuss it than to actually go through it. Whether physical or in the spiritual realm, death on any level is painful. There is no such thing as the cross without pain. Jesus said to take up our cross, and follow Him. In *The Amplified Bible* translation, it reads as follows:

> And Jesus called [to Him] the throng with His disciples and said to them, If anyone intends to come after Me, let him deny himself [forget, ignore, disown, and lose sight of himself and his own interests] and take up his cross, and [joining Me as a disciple and siding with My party] follow with Me [continually, cleaving steadfastly to Me].
>
> MARK 8:34

Just as the caterpillar must go through change to be transformed into a butterfly, so we must go through changes that require a type of death. When these changes God desires to see in us begin to take place, they are painful. As the caterpillar appears to find a place to hide in silence, God also provides for us.

Dying to self can be a messy business; it is not something we can share with everyone we know. I believe God assigns to each of us what I call "silent years." These are years when God has us hidden, and He is doing a great work in us. He is changing us into His image so we can live for His glory.

The Silent Years

As I have studied the Bible, I have learned that most of the men and women whom God used greatly had to go through some silent years. This was a period of time in their lives when God seemed to hide them away while He worked in them and made changes in their character that would be necessary for their future assignment. They entered into these periods of time one way and came out transformed.

For example, Moses was a man who felt the call of God on his life, but he had been taking matters into his own hands. He saw one of his brethren, a Hebrew, being mistreated and killed the Egyptian mistreating him. God did not lead Moses to take this action; he acted emotionally. His heart attitude may have been right — he did not want to see innocent people mistreated — but his timing was wrong. Being out of God's timing is equivalent to being out of His will. Before Moses could be used by God, he had some hard lessons to learn.

When his actions were discovered and he was confronted, Moses fled from Egypt in fear, another action God did not direct him to take. We can see from this one example that Moses was impatient and fearful, character traits that would need to be removed before God could do the great thing with Moses He had planned.

Moses fled to the wilderness, and there he spent forty years. He married and had children, but I am sure he also had a lot of time to spend with God during these "silent years." His destiny was to lead the children of Israel out of bondage into the Promised Land, and here he was in the wilderness herding sheep. I am sure that did not seem to make much sense to Moses any more than some of the places we find ourselves seem to make sense to us.

The Bible does not give a detailed account of those years; they were apparently years in which things took place between God and Moses that were private and probably painful. Moses had left everything he was familiar with, his family and friends. I am sure it seemed to him that he was moving away from what he felt called to do. Little did he know that he was being prepared for it.

When Moses went into the wilderness, we might say that he was "full of himself." He was self-assured, self-confident and self-acting. When God appeared to Moses in the burning bush and told him he was chosen to lead the people of Israel out of bondage, we see a totally different man. Now he was so humble, so broken, that God had to get angry to get him moving in faith. (See Exodus chapters 2-4.) The Bible says in Numbers 12:3, **Now the man Moses was very meek (gentle, kind, and humble) or above all the men on the face of the earth.** Just imagine — he had gone into the wilderness full of himself and his plans, and he came out the meekest man on the face of the earth. Meekness is not weakness; it is strength under control. He had strength previously, but it was not controlled. He was emotionally driven, but now we see a different man. He was strong but would not move unless he knew for sure that God was behind his actions.

You might say that he had been changed from a caterpillar to a butterfly or from a tadpole to a frog. In other words, he had definitely changed; he was transformed!

ABRAHAM, JOSEPH, JOHN THE BAPTIST AND JESUS

We see the same principle in the life of Abraham. Genesis 12 teaches us that a man named Abram was called by God to leave his family, his home and all he was familiar with and go to a place God would show him.

Just imagine — he left everything, not even knowing where he was supposed to go. As a result of his radical obedience, God made some very radical promises to him — promises of blessing, wealth, fame, leadership, descendants and so on. God entered into covenant with Abraham, telling him that if he would believe, it would be counted unto him as right standing with God, and he would be taken care of in every way.

Abraham believed God! What a great statement. That is all God is asking any of us to do: "Believe." Not just *for* things, but *through* things. Abraham was believing God for a child that would be his heir, but he had to believe God "through" some difficult and lengthy things before he saw the manifestation of the promised child. You might say that those years of waiting were his "silent years."

During those years we also see Abram (Abraham's name before God changed it, as we see in Genesis 17:5, to mean **father of a multitude** because God made him **the father of many nations**) taking action that was not God-inspired when he followed his wife's advice and took her concubine to be his secondary wife. They were tired of waiting for the promise, so they took matters into their own hands. She became pregnant by Abram and gave birth to Ishmael. Although Abram loved Ishmael, he was not the promised child and eventually brought great pain to Abram and difficulty into his life.

There are times in our lives when God simply lets us go our own way so we can learn by experience that "our way" does not work. We suffer during these years. We experience confusion, frustration and every kind of misery; however, we eventually emerge out of the cocoon of our suffering changed. We are finally ready to do things God's way! (Genesis, in chapters 12-17, tells the story of Abraham I have just shared.)

What about Joseph? He was a young man who had a dream from God. He impetuously shared his dream with his brothers, who were jealous and hated him for it. They sold him into slavery and told his father that a wild animal killed him.

Joseph was taken to Egypt and spent many difficult years there. He was lied to, lied about and imprisoned for a crime he did not commit; yet, in all of this, God had a plan. The Bible tells us about the things he went through outwardly, but we don't know, nor can we imagine, what he went through inwardly. The pain we have inside is much worse than the pain of our circumstance.

It may come from years of not understanding what is happening or why or from people who misunderstand us and judge us critically. We start out thinking, "I only want to do the will of God. Why is it so difficult?" Yet, we don't realize at that stage of metamorphosis that we are still tadpoles and caterpillars. We may say that we want to do the right thing, but our character flaws would prevent us from doing it. God must change us; there is no other way. It is painful, but a process that eventually brings freedom and joy. Like Jesus, we must endure the cross for the joy of the prize that is set before us.

We face many tests that we must pass during the silent years. Just think about how many people Joseph had to forgive, how willing he had to be to not become bitter and resentful as the years passed by and it seemed he had been forgotten. But SUDDENLY things began to change drastically.

Joseph had a reputation of being able to interpret dreams. The Pharaoh had a dream that troubled him and asked for Joseph. God gave Joseph wisdom; he delivered an accurate interpretation and the king promoted him to chief steward over all his possessions. A famine was coming, and God had Joseph trained and in position to be used to keep multitudes of people alive during this time in history. Joseph endured silent years — he passed difficult tests — but in the end he got promoted, and so does everyone else who refuses to give up.

John the Baptist also had silent years. In Luke chapter 1 we read about the birth of John. Verse 80 of that chapter tells us, **And the little boy grew and became strong in spirit; and he was in the deserts (wilderness) until the day of his appearing to Israel [the commencement of his public ministry].**

We really know nothing about John from the time of his birth to the beginning of his ministry described in Luke 3:2, except that he spent many years living in the wilderness. I believe these were the years that the Holy Spirit trained John for his future. His ministry was short but powerful. It was a special time in history; everything had to be right. I believe that the more intense our training is the greater our destiny will be.

Much the same is true of Jesus Himself. After His birth, except for His circumcision and dedication in the temple in Jerusalem when He was only eight days old (Luke 2:7-39), we read nothing more about Him until He was twelve years old. (Luke 2:41-51.)

Then from the time He was twelve years of age until He was about thirty years of age, almost nothing at all is recorded about Him. All the Bible says about Him during those silent years is that He grew and increased in favor with both God and man. (Verses 40,52.)

The statement **the child grew** says a lot. The passage of Hebrews 5:8,9 teaches us that He learned obedience through what He suffered, and His completed experience made Him perfectly equipped to become the Author and Source of eternal salvation. In His humanity Jesus had to learn, to grow, to suffer and gain experience, just as we do. He never sinned as we do, but He has gone before us as our Pioneer. He goes first, and we follow. He shows us the way to victory. THE ONLY WAY OUT IS THROUGH! We cannot run from difficult things; we must face them confidently, knowing God is by our side and will never leave us or forsake us. Even when we don't feel His Presence, we know He is with us.

During these years, I believe all of these men, as well as Jesus, spent a lot of time in praise and worship. They worshiped in the wilderness, and it helped them get to the Promised Land. In other words, if we will worship God when life does not feel good, we will see the promises of God manifest in our life. I believe that how we behave in the wilderness determines how long we will have to stay there.

THE SILENT YEARS IN MY LIFE

I am no different than you or any of the people we have just read about. God had to deal with me, and it was painful. It was not quick. In fact, it took much longer than I expected or planned on and was much more painful than I would have ever thought I could have endured.

It was exciting the day God called me into ministry, but I did not realize what I would have to go through in order to be prepared for the call. Had I known, I might not have said yes. I suppose this is the reason that God hides certain things from us and gives us the grace for each of them as we go through them. There are some things we just don't need to know ahead of time. We only need to know that God has said He will never allow more to come upon us than we can bear.

I may look good to people now when I come out on the platform in my conferences to minister to others. But you should have seen what I was like during the silent years, while I was being prepared for this ministry. I can tell you, it was not a pretty sight.

I certainly was not always a woman of faith. I experienced many emotional ups and downs — lots of anger when things didn't go my way. It was very difficult for me to learn to be submissive to authority. I did not start out with many of the fruit of the Spirit operating through me. The seed was in my spirit but had to be developed. We must always remember that gifts are given but fruit must be developed.

We can have a gift that can take us somewhere but no character to keep us there if we don't submit to God's training camp.

Before I was on international radio and television, before many people knew who I was, I experienced "silent years," years during which I had my dream and vision from God, but no big doors were opening for me. I had little opportunities, but

I did not have a little vision; therefore, most of the time I was frustrated and unthankful for what I was being allowed to do.

Oh, yes, I needed a lot of changing and still do, but at least I understand the process now. I feel very sorry for people who fight God all of their life, never understanding what He is really trying to do. We must trust Him in the hard times. We must worship in the wilderness, not just the Promised Land. The Israelites worshiped God after they crossed the Red Sea and were safe. They sang and danced. They sang the right song but on the wrong side of the river. God wants to hear our praise before we experience victory. If He doesn't, we may never experience victory at all.

I had years when the devil told me over and over that I was crazy, that I was not called by God and that I would make a fool of myself and fail. He assured me that nothing I did would bear good fruit. He told me that the suffering would never end, the pain would never stop. He told me that I was a fool for believing in something I could not see.

God gave me the grace to press on and little by little, from glory to glory. I changed, and things in my life changed in a corresponding manner. I have discovered that God releases to us what we are able to handle properly. I have come to a place in my life where I don't want anything He does not want for me. If I ask for something that He knows I cannot handle properly, I pray that He does not give it to me. The worst condition that man can ever be in is to have something God has not prepared him to handle.

I have changed. Sometimes I can barely even remember what I used to be like. I know it was extremely unpleasant.

Today that person I used to be is like someone I once knew a long, long time ago. When the silent years were over, I was glad for the work that God had done in me by His grace. I didn't like them while I was in them, nor did I understand them, but I wouldn't be who I am today or where I am without them.

THE REST OF GOD

So then, there is still awaiting a full and complete Sabbath-rest reserved for the [true] people of God;

For he who has once entered [God's] rest also has ceased from [the weariness and pain] of human labors, just as God rested from those labors peculiarly His own.

HEBREWS 4:9,10

The material I read about metamorphosis described the stages that follow after the caterpillar spins a cocoon behind a piece of loose bark or something else it uses to hide. It goes into a resting stage, and a big change begins to take place. The caterpillar is gradually changed into an adult and emerges as a brand new creature.

If you are troubled and upset, worried and worn out about all the changes that need to be made in you, why not enter the rest of God? Struggling won't change you — neither will frustration or worry. The more you rest in God the faster you will see change. If the canvas struggled under the artist's paint brush, the painting would never get finished. The canvas is perfectly still, totally submitted to the artist's wisdom and creativity. That is exactly the way we must be with God. He knows what He is doing and how to do it. We should believe in Him and enter His rest.

Stop warring with your own flesh all the time. Enter the rest of God and say, "Lord, I can't change myself. If You can't change me, nobody can. I place myself entirely in Your hands, and I wait upon You to make the changes that You know need to be made in me. Father God, I not only trust Your ways but Your timing as well." Then you can enjoy fellowship with God; you can rest in His loving arms.

The process of metamorphosis is going to hurt. Let it hurt. The more you fight it the longer it takes and the worse the pain seems. A pregnant woman trying to give birth is always told to relax and breathe. Each pain that comes brings the actual birth closer, but with each pain, she is reminded to relax and breathe. Even though change hurts, it is better than living in constant misery and discouragement. Let God do whatever it is He needs and wants to do in you.

Tell Him, "Lord, when You have finished with me, I don't even want to recognize myself. I don't want to act or be like anything that I can remember from my past. I don't want to act like the old me. I want to manifest the new creation that comes through the new birth."

DO YOU WORSHIP OR WORRY?

Looking away [from all that will distract] to Jesus, Who is the Leader and the Source of our faith [giving the first incentive for our belief] and is also its Finisher [bringing it to maturity and perfection]. . . .

HEBREWS 12:2

Sometimes we have trouble seeing anything good in our life. It is because we are looking at the wrong thing. We look too much at what is wrong with us. The Bible does not tell us to look to ourselves; it tells us to look to Christ. The message is "look and live."

In Numbers 21 we see that when the Israelites were out in the wilderness, they were dying in large numbers because of a plague of snakes that had come upon them as a result of their sin. Moses went and fell down before God and worshiped Him. He turned his attention immediately to God, not to himself or anyone else, to solve the problem.

I have discovered that throughout the Bible when people had a problem, they worshiped. At least the ones who were victorious did. They didn't worry — they worshiped.

I would ask you today: *Do you worry or worship?*

Moses sought God about how to handle the snakes. He didn't make his own plan and ask God to bless it; he didn't try to reason out an answer, nor did he worry — he worshiped. His action brought a response from God.

And the Lord said to Moses, Make a fiery serpent [of bronze] and set it on a pole; and everyone who is bitten, when he looks at it, shall live.

NUMBERS 21:8

We know that the pole with the bronze serpent on it represented the cross and Jesus taking our sin upon Himself on it. The message is still the same today: "Look and live." Look at

Jesus, at what He has done, not at yourself and what you have done or can do.

The answer to your problem, whatever it may be, is not worry, but worship. Begin to worship God because He is good, and His goodness will be released in your life. Remember, the battle belongs to the Lord.

Chapter

12

Continue to Behold and Worship

And all of us, as with unveiled face, [because we] continued to behold [in the Word of God] as in a mirror the glory of the Lord, are constantly being transfigured into His very own image in ever increasing splendor and from one degree of glory to another; [for this comes] from the Lord [Who is] the Spirit.

2 CORINTHIANS 3:18

This verse tells us that we are constantly being transfigured into the Lord's image. How? By continuing to behold Him.

The word *behold* means "to gaze upon,"[1] "to fix the eyes upon"[2] something, rather than to glance at something. What we need to do is stare at Jesus and glance at our problems, not stare at our problems and glance at Jesus occasionally.

I would venture to say that most people spend more time thinking about what they have done wrong than they ever spend thinking about what Jesus has done right. Remember that what Jesus did, He did for us. He took our place, took the punishment we deserved. He became our Substitute. These are the things we should meditate on.

CONTINUE TO BEHOLD

Then said Jesus to those Jews which believed on him, If ye continue in my word, then are ye my disciples indeed;

And ye shall know the truth, and the truth shall make you free.

JOHN 8:31,32 KJV

Second Corinthians 3:18 says that we are transfigured as we *continue* to behold Jesus in the Word. If we expect to be transfigured into the image of our Lord, we must understand the principle of "continuing."

Continuing requires a long-term commitment. It means we are in for the long haul so to speak. We are not just "trying" something for a week to see if we get good results, and if we don't, we go back to our old ways. We must study the Word until God's truth becomes revelation to us. When it becomes alive and real on the inside of us, it begins to make a difference in our daily lives.

There are several encouragements in God's Word not to give up. Galatians 6:9 teaches us not to become weary in well doing, for we shall reap if we do not faint and give up. We must continue; we must remain and be steadfast. We must continue through hard times. We must endure difficulty, realizing that we grow during hard times. We receive God's promises as a result of faith and patience, not just faith by itself. We must be patient through the changes in our life. Another word for *patience* is *long-suffering.* That word means exactly what it says; it means to suffer long. Discipline is a must!

If we truly want to be transformed, transfigured, changed into the image of God, we must continue to study His Word and worship Him.

Let me give you a couple of examples.

CONTINUE TO WORSHIP

In his book *Worship — Unleashing the Supernatural Power of God in Your Life,* Norvel Hayes tells an awesome story about a man in Hawaii who came to him for counseling.[3]

This man told Norvel that he had three children and hadn't had a job in two years. He was $15,000 in debt and had tried everything he knew to make money.

This man owned some big equipment, which he had been using to harvest sugar cane. But some large corporations had come in and taken over the sugar cane business so this man's equipment had sat idle for two years.

The man said that he didn't have any money for food for his children so he had had to go on food stamps. He said he had borrowed all the money he could from his friends, but he could not borrow any more. So he was asking Norvel for help.

Norvel told this man, "You need to start worshiping the Lord every morning. Learn to praise Him with your mouth. Before you start believing God to work in your behalf, you have got to start thanking Him for all that He is. Spend time worshiping Him every day. Look to Him in worship and praise. Give Him thanks for all He has done for you."

Later, Norvel met that same man, and he told Norvel that he and his wife had worshiped the Lord the way Norvel had told him to do for five months, but nothing had happened.

Then one morning in the fifth month, as this man was getting up off his knees after worshiping God, he received a telephone call. It was from one of the large corporations that had put him out of business. Now they were asking him to do some work for them using his equipment for a period of six weeks. They offered to pay him $80,000 for the job. Before the six weeks were over, he received from the same company another contract worth another $80,000.

The man went on to say that worshiping and praising God had brought him out of debt in a year's time and that he had $40,000 in his savings account and another $80,000 job coming up.

Later, Norvel learned from the man's pastor that just a year and a half after he had started worshiping God, this man's tithe to the church was $65,000!

And it had all happened, Norvel said, because this man had heard the truth and was willing to act on it by taking time to seek the Lord, to bow down before Him and worship and praise Him. We should also take notice that the man *continued* in worship for five months and still nothing had happened. Then SUDDENLY his victory came. What if the man had given up in the fourth month? That is what many people do. They give up just a little too soon and never see the awesome things God had planned for them.

WE WORSHIP THROUGH TITHES AND OFFERINGS

In the early years of my relationship with God, He dealt with my husband and me to begin giving more and more. What we had didn't increase; it actually decreased for a period of time. We went through six years of really hard times with our finances.

I still remember when I transitioned from just trying something to being determined to continue, no matter how long it took.

One day a friend of mine came by and, in the course of our conversation, began telling me about several ways the Lord was blessing their family financially. I wanted to be happy for them, but at the same time I wondered why we were still struggling. I could feel discouragement settling on me like a cloud. I went and lay down on our daughter's bed and began to cry quite vehemently about our financial situation when suddenly something rose up inside me, and I made a decision. I said, "God, we are going to give and do what Your Word says until You come back to get us. Even if we never see one result, we are continuing. We are going to do it to honor You, just because You said in Your Word to do it. The results are not our problem; they are Yours!

Once Dave and I made that decision, our commitment closed the door that had been open to the devil, which allowed him to torment us. We began to prosper after that day and have continued to this day.

We were worshiping God with our giving. Worship in any form is not just another method to follow to get the blessings of God activated in your life. God knows our hearts, and our motives must be pure. We cannot do the right thing just to get right results. We must learn to do the right thing because it is right. A righteous man does right because he cannot do anything else. He leaves the results with God, and they always turn out good. There will be a time of testing, but those who continue will always reap.

I am urging you to worship instead of worry. Make a decision to continue no matter how long it takes, and you will see positive changes take place in your life and in yourself.

THIS IS FROM THE LORD

You and I can feel sorry for ourselves, run to everyone we know for counseling, rebuke the devil, ask for prayer and do everything else we can think of, but if we don't worship God, we are leaving out the most important part.

The Bible says that we must *continue* to behold, in the Word of God, as in a mirror, the glory of the Lord. If we will do that continually, we will constantly be transfigured or transformed into His very own image in ever-increasing splendor and from one degree of glory to another degree of glory.

Where does all this come from? The answer is found at the end of 2 Corinthians 3:18: . . . [for this comes] from the Lord [Who is] the Spirit.

This transformation is not something we do; . . . **this is the Lord's doing, and it is marvelous in our eyes** (Matthew 21:42).

Chapter

13

God Is for Us!

===

What then shall we say to [all] this? If God is for us, who [can be]
against us? [Who can be our foe, if God is on our side?]

ROMANS 8:31

God is a big God; nothing is impossible with Him, and He is on our side. We have nothing to fear from our enemies because none of them are as great as our God.

God is for us; He is on our side. The devil has one position — he is against us. But God is over us, under us, through us, for us, and He surrounds us.

The Bible says, **Those who trust in, lean on, and confidently hope in the Lord are like Mount Zion, which cannot be moved but abides and stands fast forever. As the mountains are round about Jerusalem, so the Lord is round about His people from this time forth and forever (Psalm 125:1,2).**

So like Mount Zion, we should not be moved because God is all around us. And if that wasn't enough, I saved the best until last: He is in us, and He said that He will never leave us or forsake us.

So if the devil is only against us, but God is with us, over us, under us, around us and in us, I would say that we are in very good condition. Of whom, then, should we be afraid?

Fear the Lord, Not Man

*Let those now who reverently and worshipfully fear the Lord say
that His mercy and loving-kindness endure forever.*

*Out of my distress I called upon the Lord; the Lord answered me
and set me free and in a large place.*

The Lord is on my side; I will not fear. What can man do to me?

PSALM 118:4-6

In the first verse of this passage, when the psalmist says, "I
will reverence and worship God, saying that His mercy and
loving-kindness endure forever," what is he doing? He is worshiping God for some of His attributes, as we have discussed. He
is praising God for His mercy and His loving-kindness.

It builds faith in us when we meditate on and talk about the
great attributes of God.

In the next verse he tells how, in his distress, he called upon
the Lord. But notice that he did not do that until after he had
first worshiped the Lord and praised Him for the very attributes
he was calling upon Him to display in his distressing situation.

Finally, in the third verse of this passage the psalmist
declares, **The Lord is on my side; I will not fear.** Why should
we fear? If Almighty God is for me, and He is, then what can
mere man do to me? We definitely need to realize how big God
is and how small our enemies are when compared to Him.

You may be worried about what man is going to do to you.
You may be worried that man is going to take your job away,
that man is not going to give you what you need. Man may treat

you unfairly or may reject you. You may be worried about what man is going to think or say about you.

If so, you need to understand that it is insulting to God when we are more concerned about people than we are about Him.

The Bible tells us that we are not to fear man, but that we are to reverently and worshipfully fear the Lord. When we refuse to fear man, but instead reverently and worshipfully fear the Lord, then God moves in our behalf so that nothing that man tries to do to us ever permanently harms us. They may come against us one way, but they will have to flee before us seven ways. (Deuteronomy 28:7.)

For a period of time it may seem as if someone is taking advantage of us. But if we keep our eyes on God and continue to worship Him, keeping our conversation in line with His Word, in the end God will reward us and will bring justice because He is a God of Justice. He loves Justice and hates wrongdoing.

We prolong our trouble when we try to make people give us what we think is due us. We should not do that. Instead, we should wait on the Lord, and let Him bring us what we are supposed to have. God is our Vindicator. We cannot vindicate ourselves, and we actually make matters worse when we try to.

It seems we worry a lot that somebody is going to take advantage of us. We need to retire from self-care and cast our care upon the Lord. If we have our eyes on God, nobody is going to take advantage of us — at least not for very long. God has thousands of ways to get His blessings to us. When a door closes, He opens another one. If there are no doors, He makes one. This is why our position should be, "If God is for me, who can be against me?"

WHAT CAN MAN DO?

The Word of God is filled with promises that God will take care of us. One of those promises is stated so beautifully that I don't see how we can read it and remain fearful.

> . . . . *for He [God] Himself has said, I will not in any way fail you nor give you up nor leave you without support. [I will] not, [I will] not, [I will] not in any degree leave you helpless nor forsake nor let [you] down (relax My hold on you)! [Assuredly not!]*

> *So we take comfort and are encouraged and confidently and boldly say, The Lord is my Helper; I will not be seized with alarm [I will not fear or dread or be terrified]. What can man do to me?*

> HEBREWS 13:5,6

These Scriptures are very comforting to me. They are emphatic, stating three times that God will not leave us helpless. When the Lord says something once, we should believe He is serious. But saying it three times is placing a strong emphasis on His promise to never leave us without support. I encourage you to meditate on these Scriptures anytime fear comes against your mind concerning your future or what man will do to you. The Word of God has inherent power, and simply meditating on it makes you feel better. Faith comes by hearing God's Word. When Satan presents fear, run to the Word of God. The fear of man can cause us to lose our destiny.

In the Old Testament Saul feared the people more than he feared God, and it caused him to lose the kingship. (1 Samuel 13:8-14.) Saul did not fulfill his destiny due to fear.

Saul was destined to rule and reign with God, just as we are. The New Testament teaches us that we are all kings and priests unto our God. God has a place of blessing in mind for each of us. He wants us to rule, not be ruled by fear and intimidation. But, like Saul, we can lose the kingship, our rightful position of ruling and reigning, if we fear man instead of God.

REVERENT FEAR OF GOD

But as for me, I will enter Your house through the abundance of Your steadfast love and mercy; I will worship toward and at Your holy temple in reverent fear and awe of You.

PSALM 5:7

When we talk about fearing God, we are not talking about a wrong kind of fear. We are talking about that reverential fear that causes us to bow in His Presence and even to prostrate ourselves before Him and say, "My God, there is none like You; Whom shall I fear? If You are for me, what can man do to me?"

Even the apostle Paul said in Galatians 1:10, **Now am I trying to win the favor of men, or of God? Do I seek to please men? If I were still seeking popularity with men, I should not be a bond servant of Christ (the Messiah).**

That is a Scripture that has always gripped my heart because I know how rejection from man has tried to prevent me from going forward with the call of God on my life.

Have you ever been attacked by rejection? Of course you have; we all have. It is the devil's way of trying to keep us from going forward. He knows that we will be blessed if we are in the will of God so he uses the fear of man's rejection to hold us back.

When I was filled with the Holy Spirit in 1976, I lost most of my friends, was asked to leave my church and was ostracized by family members, who thought we were being deceived. It got even worse when God called me to teach and preach His Word. Everywhere I turned, I was being rejected by someone I loved and cared about. It was very difficult to go on. Many times I wanted to give in to the pressure and make decisions that would please people. I look back now and shudder to think what I might have sacrificed had I bowed down to the pressure.

There were other very important times in my life and ministry when the devil launched attacks of rejection against me, and each of them came at a time when God was trying to promote me into the next level of what he had for my life.

Anyone who is going to do the will of God must have more fear of God than man. I wanted acceptance, but I did not want to be out of the will of God, and I knew I would be if I did what my friends wanted me to do. I thank God for His grace that sustained and strengthened me during those difficult testing times.

Anyone who is going to do God's will must remember what Jesus told His disciples: "A servant is not above his master. If they hate Me, they are going to hate you; if they persecute Me, they are going to persecute you." (John 13:16; 15:20.) But He also told them, "If they reject you, in effect they are rejecting Me." In other words, the Lord takes it personally when people reject you because you are trying to do the right thing, and He is your Vindicator; your reward comes from Him.

The Lord wants you and me to be released from the bondage of the fear of man and the fear of rejection. He knows that we are never going to be all He wants us to be if we have that fear in us. We need to care more about what He thinks than we do about what people think — because He is our Provider; man is not.

Chapter

14

God Will Provide

Praise the Lord! (Hallelujah!) I will praise and give thanks to the Lord with my whole heart in the council of the upright and in the congregation.

The works of the Lord are great, sought out by all those who have delight in them.

His work is honorable and glorious, and His righteousness endures forever.

He has made His wonderful works to be remembered; the Lord is gracious, merciful, and full of loving compassion.

He has given food and provision to those who reverently and worshipfully fear Him; He will remember His covenant forever and imprint it [on His mind].

PSALM 111:1-5

A re you perhaps concerned at this point in your life about provision? Are you in need of provision in some area, and you are not really sure where it is going to come from?

Surveys I have conducted in conferences show that at least 50 percent of people are in fear concerning where their provision will come from.

Notice again the last verse in the above passage in which the psalmist is praising and worshiping God for His great works on behalf of His people: **He has given food and provision to those who reverently and worshipfully fear Him; He will remember His covenant forever and imprint it [on His mind]** (verse 5).

This is telling us that as long as we worship God, we are going to have His provision. We continually see the same theme in God's Word — worship wins the battle!

Mark that verse in your Bible; meditate on it, even memorize it because it holds the key to the meeting of all your needs. That way when a need arises in your life, you will have hidden the Word of God in your heart, and it will strengthen you and help you remain in faith rather than fear.

Perhaps you have been told that you are going to lose your job or housing. Maybe you are elderly and living on Social Security, and you wonder about what is going to happen to you in the future. You see prices on everything rising all the time, and the devil whispers in your ear, "You are not going to have enough to live on." Or maybe the figures just don't add up; your income simply is not enough to support you, and yet you're doing all you know to do.

Whatever the reason for your concern about your provision, take this verse and digest it. Jeremiah said, **Your words were found, and I ate them; and Your words were to me a joy and the rejoicing of my heart** . . . (Jeremiah 15:16). We must, so to speak, "chew" on the Word of God. In his writings the psalmist uses the word *selah*, which means **pause, and calmly think of that** (AMP), to encourage the reader to slowly digest what has been said. Often we read for quantity and should read for quality. Read in a manner that allows the Word to go down into your innermost part and feed you.

That Word says that God gives food and provision to those who reverently fear Him and worship Him. That means that whatever your situation may be, God will provide for you as long as you are worshiping and magnifying Him.

Worshiping is actually fun and energizing; worry makes our hearts heavy and causes a loss of joy. Worship; don't worry! The battle belongs to the Lord.

WORSHIP IS WISDOM

The reverent fear and worship of the Lord is the beginning of Wisdom. . . .

PSALM 111:10

If you will read the book of Proverbs and look at all the radical promises that are made to the person who walks in wisdom, and then realize that reverence and worship are the beginning of wisdom, you will quickly see why reverence and worship are so important.

The Bible says that those who walk in wisdom will be wealthy. They will live a long life. They will be exceedingly happy. They will be blessed, so blessed that they will be envied. (Proverbs 3:1-18.)

But there is no such thing as wisdom without worship. Many people today are seeking knowledge, and knowledge is good, but wisdom is better. Wisdom is the right use of knowledge. Knowledge without wisdom can cause one to be puffed up, or filled with pride, which will ultimately ruin his life. A wise person will always be knowledgeable, but not all knowledgeable people are wise.

I believe that in our society today, we exalt knowledge more than we should. Education seems to be most people's main goal, and yet our world today is rapidly declining morally. Education is good, but it is not better than wisdom. God's Word tells us to cry out for wisdom; seek it as we would silver and gold; make it a vital necessity in life. There is nothing more important than wisdom, and the beginning of it is reverence and worship.

The worshiper will be taught wisdom by God.

THERE IS NO WANT IN WORSHIP

The Angel of the Lord encamps around those who fear Him [who revere and worship Him with awe] and each of them He delivers.

O taste and see that the Lord [our God] is good! Blessed (happy, fortunate, to be envied) is the man who trusts and takes refuge in Him.

O fear the Lord, you His saints [revere and worship Him]! For there is no want to those who truly revere and worship Him with godly fear.

PSALM 34:7-9

Do you want your angels to go to work in your life? Then start worshiping God because the Bible says that His angel camps around those who revere and worship Him to watch over them and deliver them. It is really amazing how many promises are made to those who worship.

Do you want to be sure that all of your needs will be met? Then start worshiping God because the Bible says that there is no want, no lack, to those who truly revere and worship the Lord with godly fear.

"Well, if all that is so, why isn't God moving in my life?" you may ask.

I believe that God is moving in your life. I believe that He is doing great things in your life. He is doing great things in all of our lives, if we would only see them. Often we spend our time counting up what we don't have instead of what we do have. We think about what we have lost instead of what we have left. This prevents us from realizing how truly blessed we are.

Having a thankful heart is part of worship, and it certainly is the attitude of a "worshiper." God does a lot with a little, and He does the most with nothing. He has created the world we see out of nothing. He uses nothings and nobodies to do His work through, according to 1 Corinthians chapter 1. So even if we had nothing, we could give our nothing to God, and He would do something with it. God has no problem providing us with whatever we need in this life. If we will only worship Him, cast our care upon Him and obey his instructions to us, we will always have our needs met abundantly.

I have lost a lot in my life. I was abused in my childhood so I never really had the opportunity to be a child. For a long time I really resented what I had lost. I resented the lost years that I could never get back; I resented not having a good start in life because I knew a lot of my problems as an adult stemmed from my wrong beginning in life.

Finally, I saw that I could not do anything about what I had lost, and I started looking at what I had left. For one thing, I had the rest of my life, and so do you. Even if the years you have lived haven't been pleasant, you still have your future.

I began to worship God right where I was at, and I trusted Him to be faithful to His Word. I gave Him what I had left. I said, "Lord, here I am. I am not much, but if You can use me, I'm Yours."

I encourage you to begin to worship God right where you are at; worship Him for what you do have, and forget about what you don't have. There is no want in worship. As we worship God, He meets all of our needs.

PRAISE SAVES

I love You fervently and devotedly, O Lord, my Strength.

The Lord is my Rock, my Fortress, and my Deliverer; my God, my keen and firm Strength in Whom I will trust and take refuge, my Shield, and the Horn of my salvation, my High Tower.

I will call upon the Lord, Who is to be praised; so shall I be saved from my enemies.

PSALM 18:1-3

What did the psalmist say he would do to be saved from his enemies? . . . **call upon the Lord, Who is to be praised.**

If you and I will go past the gates of praise into God's Presence and begin to worship Him there, our enemies will get so confused, they will begin to attack each other.

We saw that happen to Jehoshaphat's and Gideon's enemies.

When the devil tries to upset us, and we react by singing praise to God, it confuses him and his demons so badly that they begin to attack one another. And in the process we find new a level of joy.

As we have seen, there is too much fear among God's people. But the Lord says to us, **Fear not, for I am with you.**

Under the Old Covenant, God is just with His people — and look at the awesome victories they were given. But we can go far beyond that because the same God Who led the Israelites to victory after victory over their enemies is not only *with* us, He is also *in* those of us who are Christians.

I like to think that He is as close to me as my breath, and I need Him just as much as I need each breath to live. God is our life. As Paul said, **For in Him we live and move and have our being** . . . (Acts 17:28). God is everything, and He is worthy of our praise and worship.

Chapter
15

God Is on My Side!

=====

Little children, you are of God [you belong to Him] and have [already] defeated and overcome them [the agents of the antichrist], because He Who lives in you is greater (mightier) than he who is in the world.

1 JOHN 4:4

People have so many fears that we could spend all day naming them and probably not run out of things that people fear.

Many believers have the same fears that everyone else has. That is why Scriptures like 1 John 4:4 were given to us — to assure us that because of the Presence and Power of Almighty God within us, we have nothing to fear.

When you start to be afraid, you ought to open your Bible, read that verse out loud and say, "Satan, I don't have to be afraid of you because God's Word says that I have already defeated you. Satan, God is your greatest nightmare, and He is on my side!"

Do you know what the Bible means when it says that you and I are more than conquerors through Jesus Christ? I really believe that it means that we don't have to live in fear. Before the battle even begins, we have already been told that we will win it. We know the outcome — we know we are going to *come out* victorious!

We may not like having to go through the battle; resisting fear may not always be easy. But we can be encouraged, knowing that what the devil means for our harm, God intends for our good.

If God is on our side, and if we are on His side, in the end everything is going to work out for our good because whoever is with the Lord is going to win. That is an established scriptural fact. God's side is the winning side!

"BUT GOD . . ."

But God shows and clearly proves His [own] love for us by the fact that while we were still sinners, Christ (the Messiah, the Anointed One) died for us.

ROMANS 5:8

There is a little phrase in the Bible that I get excited about every time I come across it. It is just two little words, but it is found throughout the Bible and is probably one of the most powerful two-word phrases in it.

It is simply this: **But God. . . .**

As we go through the Bible, we constantly read disastrous reports of the terrible things the devil had planned for God's people. Then we come to this little phrase, **But God . . .**, and the next thing we read about is a victory.

In the above Scripture, the fact is mentioned that we are all sinners, a condition that deserves punishment and death. The phrase **But God . . .** interrupts the process. God's love is brought into the situation and changes everything. While we were sinners, Christ died for us, and by doing so, proved His love for us. He proved that His love interrupts the devastation of sin.

Here is another wonderful example of how God interrupts the evil plan Satan has for us.

And the patriarchs [Jacob's sons], boiling with envy and hatred and anger, sold Joseph into slavery in Egypt; but God was with him,

And delivered him from all his distressing afflictions and won him goodwill and favor and wisdom and understanding in the sight of Pharaoh, king of Egypt, who made him governor over Egypt and all his house.

ACTS 7:9,10

Satan had planned to destroy Joseph through filling his brothers' hearts with hatred and envy. They sold him into slavery, thinking that they were rid of Joseph once and for all, **but God** had another plan. God interrupted Satan's plan and brought tremendous blessing into Joseph's life.

That is the way it is meant to be in our daily lives. For example, one of the stories might go something like this: You had a job for ten years and thought it was going to be your future, and then the company folded, and it looked like your future was destroyed. **But God** . . . can put you into a job that is far better than the one you had. God can even give you favor and help you get a job you're not even qualified for in the natural and then give you grace to do the job properly. He can enable you to do something that nobody in the world would have ever thought you were capable of doing, including yourself.

I had a very similar situation take place in my own life.

In the 1970s, I had a job working in the downtown area of St. Louis, Missouri, which is our hometown. My husband, Dave, also worked downtown, which meant we were able to both get to work using our one automobile. The job was a good paying job with benefits, and I felt blessed to have it. Then a test came.

My boss, who was not a Christian, wanted me more or less to help him steal some money by being a party to deception. A customer had a credit balance on their account because they had paid an invoice twice. This meant that we owed them money. The boss didn't want them to know about the credit balance because he didn't want to give them the money back. So he told me to debit it off their account and send them a statement that month showing a zero balance instead of the actual credit balance they had.

I went home that night and agonized over the situation. My conscience clearly told me that I could not do such a thing, but at the same time I was afraid of losing my job. We had financial commitments that required me to work.

I made my decision, which was to tell my boss that I could not do what he had asked. Actually, the decision I made put me in a position of worshiping God. I may not have lifted my hands or bowed down or even said a prayer of praise or worship, but my actions were worshiping Him. I was putting God and His principles first, even if it meant that I would lose my job.

When I spoke with my boss, he became visibly angry but just told me to go back to work. I had simply told him that I was a Christian, and although I realized that he did not share my faith, I was unable to go against my conscience and help him deceive the customer. I told him that I didn't want to lose my job, but I had to do what I believed was right.

I was fully expecting all day to have him come into my office and tell me I was fired, but at the end of the day, he walked in and told me to send the customer a check. He never mentioned the situation again, and neither did I. **But God** saw to it that I continually got promoted until finally I was the second person in charge of the entire company. My situation was much like Joseph's. I was in control of everything when the boss was gone, which was quite frequently. I really did not have the education to do the job; I wasn't qualified as far as the world would look at qualifications, but I was supernaturally qualified because God opened a door and gave me grace to do the job.

What looked like a terrible situation turned out to be a great blessing because God interrupted Satan's plan of destruction.

We must learn to look at things through the eyes of faith rather than in the natural. What normally happens in a situation can be totally changed when God comes on the scene.

When God called me into the ministry, people told me, "Joyce, a group of us have been talking, and we feel that there is no way you are ever going to be able to do what you say God has told you that you are going to do. We don't feel your personality is suitable for such a job."

I still remember how awful I felt when they said those things to me. I was hurt and discouraged . . . **but God** had called me, and He qualified me. What others thought was not even useable, God saw value in. He helped me, and He will do the same thing for you.

THEY FELL ON THEIR FACES

And all the congregation cried out with a loud voice, and [they] wept that night.

All the Israelites grumbled and deplored their situation, accusing Moses and Aaron, to whom the whole congregation said, Would that we had died in Egypt! Or that we had died in this wilderness!

Why does the Lord bring us to this land to fall by the sword? Our wives and little ones will be a prey. Is it not better for us to return to Egypt?

And they said one to another, Let us choose a captain and return to Egypt.

Then Moses and Aaron fell on their faces before all the assembly of Israelites.

NUMBERS 14:1-5

Notice Moses and Aaron's reaction to the Israelites' murmuring and complaining — they fell on their faces.

This action of falling on one's face is found throughout the Bible. If all the Israelites had been on their faces, they would have seen miracle after miracle. But no, they were too busy feeling sorry for themselves, finding fault with God and Moses, talking negatively, wanting to go back to Egypt.

But thank God for Moses and Aaron. They fell on their faces and began to worship God. Their action showed reverence for God. They took this action before the whole assembly, I am sure, as an object lesson of what others should be doing.

We see another example in Genesis 17 concerning Abram. **When he was ninety-nine years old, the Lord appeared to him and said, I am the Almighty God; walk and live habitually before Me and be perfect (blameless, wholehearted, complete).** Abram responded by falling on his face. I love this example because, like us, Abram knew that he could not walk perfect before God unless God did it through him. What was impossible for him without God would become possible with God, so he worshiped. That was all he could do, but it was enough because God did the rest.

When we are faced with impossibilities, we should never give up; we should worship and watch God work in our behalf. Remember, all things are possible to those who believe.

THE LORD IS WITH US!

And Joshua son of Nun and Caleb son of Jephunneh, who were among the scouts who had searched the land, rent their clothes,

And they said to all the company of Israelites, The land through which we passed as scouts is an exceedingly good land.

If the Lord delights in us, then He will bring us into this land and give it to us, a land flowing with milk and honey.

Only do not rebel against the Lord, neither fear the people of the land, for they are bread for us. Their defense and the shadow [of protection] is removed from over them, but the Lord is with us. Fear them not.

NUMBERS 14:6-9

Joshua and Caleb were two men of God who found themselves involved in a group of people who were all negative and full of unbelief. Joshua and Caleb would not allow the negative people to adversely affect them; they remained full of faith and confidence that they could conquer their enemies. We also must be determined not to let such people steal our joy by taking away our positive attitude. Don't let them destroy your confidence and belief that God is a good God and has a good plan for your life. Satan uses people like this to drain us. Their misery and negativism must not be allowed to affect or infect our joy.

There are times in life when circumstances are not very exciting. We look and see problems that look like giants to us, but we need to remember that God is greater than the giants.

Joshua and Caleb found themselves in just such a situation. Moses had sent them and ten other men into the Promised Land of Canaan to spy out the land and bring back a report describing it. Ten of the men came back and said, "The land is full of good fruit, but it is also full of giants, and we cannot defeat them."

But Joshua and Caleb had a different attitude. They too had seen the giants but preferred to keep their eyes on God, Whom they believed was greater than the giants. Their report was, "Let us go up at once and defeat them because we are well able." The negative people immediately said, "We are not able."

This is the way it often is in life. There are always people who are positive; they are trying to go forward. Then there are negative people, who try to contaminate everything good and positive with their bad attitude. Ten of the spies were negative and two were positive. Based on those figures, that means 80 percent of the people said they were not able to defeat the giants, and only 20 percent believed God was greater than the problem. Those figures are probably fairly accurate today. If a larger percentage of people believed in the great power of God, we would see more people succeeding than we do.

Sad to say, we often get our eyes on the giants instead of on God. We lose our focus; we become entangled with the problem and lose sight of what God has called us to do. I believe that more time spent worshiping and praising God would help us keep a clear focus and enable us to go forward with a strong positive attitude, believing we can do anything God tells us to do.

Joshua and Caleb reminded the others that God had promised to give them the land. They encouraged them not to rebel against the Lord and not to fear the people. They said, "The Lord is with us!"

God is not with the enemy; He is with us. And if God is for us, who can be against us? I encourage you to practice maintaining a good attitude. Be content, thankful. Notice what God is doing, not just what you think He is not doing for you. Beware of complaining. Instead, worship God and keep worshiping Him until your breakthrough comes. Having a good attitude will bring your breakthrough quicker than being grouchy. However long we are going to have to wait, we might as well be happy while we wait. It is called "enjoying where you at on the way to where you are going."

Paul learned how to be content whether he was abased or abounding, and we can do the same thing.

Not that I am implying that I was in any personal want, for I have learned how to be content (satisfied to the point where I am not disturbed or disquieted) in whatever state I am.

PHILIPPIANS 4:11

Paul learned from experience what worked and what didn't. I have also learned and am still learning that being discontent is not worship. I try to keep in mind that it does no good at all. I try in my life to be happy no matter what is going on. I don't want to waste time being discontent. If we all wait until we have no problems to be happy, we may never get the opportunity, so let's be happy now!

Like Paul, no matter what our current circumstance is, we know that God is with us. In fact, He is actually way ahead of us. He already knows the outcome, and His plan is for our good, not for failure.

FEAR NOT — GOD GOES BEFORE YOU

Be strong, courageous, and firm; fear not nor be in terror before them, for it is the Lord your God Who goes with you; He will not fail you or forsake you.

And Moses called to Joshua and said to him in the sight of all Israel, Be strong, courageous, and firm, for you shall go with this people into the land which the Lord has sworn to their fathers to give them, and you shall cause them to possess it.

It is the Lord Who goes before you; He will [march] with you; He will not fail you or let you go or forsake you; [let there be no cowardice or flinching, but] fear not, neither become broken [in spirit] (depressed, dismayed, and unnerved with alarm).

DEUTERONOMY 31:6-8

In this passage Moses told the Israelites to be strong, courageous and firm. Do you know what it means to be firm? It means to stick to what you know is right without letting anything or anyone talk you out of it.

Moses also told Joshua that he was to be strong, courageous and firm because he was to lead the people into the land that the Lord had given them. He assured him that the Lord would never fail him or forsake him but that He would go before him to lead him to victory. As we have seen, that same promise has been made to you and me.

It is comforting to think that everywhere we go God has been there before us, preparing the way. Prior to our conferences that are held worldwide, someone always goes before us and prepares the way. They make sure all the arrangements are made properly before Dave and I arrive. For example, just recently we had a conference planned in another part of the world. When our employee arrived, he realized that the arena we had planned to use was in a part of the city that would be very difficult to get to and home from. The traffic would be heavy before and after meetings; there was only one road in and one road out; therefore, it might take us as long as four hours to get where we needed to go.

We had sent him months in advance, and it proved to be very fruitful. He was able to change the meeting place and save us a lot of time. We always send a team of people into a city at least two days before we arrive. They make sure they know all the necessary directions to get everywhere; they check the hotels and all the arrangements are made so when we arrive, we can focus on ministering to the people rather than getting entangled in details we don't need to be involved in. This actually makes our ministry much more fruitful.

This knowledge comforts me; it gives me confidence. Likewise, knowing that God has gone before me in every situation of my life gives me great confidence, and I am free to live without fear.

For example, if you have a court case coming up, you need to understand that God has already gone ahead of you into the court before you ever arrive. Or, if you need to confront your employer about some issue at work, believe what the Word says. Believe that God will go before you and prepare the way, that He will give you favor and even give you the right words to say when the time comes.

I also encourage you to be careful of your thoughts when facing situations like these. Often we pray and ask God to help us, we ask for miracles, but in our thoughts and imaginations, we see disaster and failure. Cast down all wrong imaginations and everything that does not agree with God's Word.

The psalmist David said, **Let the words of my mouth and the meditations of my heart be acceptable in Your sight, O Lord** . . . (Psalm 19:14). God is pleased with our thoughts and words when they agree with His Word.

When we need God's power to help us in a situation, we cannot ask for something positive and then speak about the situation negatively. We must ask for what we need, and then keep our thoughts and words in line with what we have asked for according to God's Word.

Believe, and you will see the glory of God!

Chapter

16

Remain in Position

*You shall not need to fight in this battle; take your positions, stand
still, and see the deliverance of the Lord [Who is] with you, O
Judah and Jerusalem. Fear not nor be dismayed. Tomorrow go out
against them, for the Lord is with you.*

2 CHRONICLES 20:17

In Ephesians 6, a chapter about spiritual warfare, we are
told that after having done all the crisis demands, we are
to stand. Then in 2 Chronicles 20 we are told that we will not
need to fight our own battles because they belong to the Lord,
not to us. All we are to do is take our position and remain in it
until we see victory.

What is our position? I believe it is worshiping God.

Like the enemies of Judah and Israel, the devil has a plan to
attack and destroy us, and he is working his plan. **But God** . . .
has a surprise for him.

A good friend of mine, who is a Greek scholar, recently sent
me his paraphrased edition of John 10:10. I would like to share
it with you. It gives a clear idea of just how determined the devil
is to kill, steal and destroy, but Jesus has another plan.

"The thief, that spiritual bandit who wants to get his hands
into every good thing in your life, this pickpocket is looking for
any opportunity to wiggle his way so deeply into your personal

affairs that he can walk off with everything that you hold precious and dear. And that's not all! When he's finished raping you of all your goods and possessions, he'll take his plan to rob you blind to the next level, by creating conditions and situations so horrible that you'll see no way to solve the problem. He'll try to put you under unbearable pressure to make you feel obligated to throw in the towel and give up everything that he hasn't already stolen from you. The goal of this thief is to totally waste and devastate your life. If nothing stops him, he'll leave you insolvent, flat broke, and cleaned out in every area of your life. You'll end up feeling as if you are finished and out of business! Make no mistake: his ultimate aim is to obliterate you!

"But I have come that they might have, keep, and constantly retain a vitality, gusto, vigor, and zest for living that springs up from deep down inside, a life that is not rattled or easily shaken by any outward events — I came that they might embrace this unrivaled, unequaled, matchless, incomparable, richly-loaded and overflowing life to the ultimate maximum!"[1]

I am so glad for those words "but I have come" (**I came** AMP), which were spoken by Jesus Himself. Once again we see that Jesus has interrupted the devil's plan.

ELIJAH PREDICTED RAIN IN DROUGHT

And Elijah said to Ahab, Go up, eat and drink, for there is the sound of abundance of rain.

1 KINGS 18:41

As I discussed earlier in the book, there had been a drought in the land for three long years, and God had already told Elijah to tell King Ahab that it was going to rain. But as of yet there was no sign of rain. In obedience Elijah told Ahab to get prepared because he heard the sound of abundance of rain.

Although I shared some things about Elijah earlier in the book, there are a few more points I want to cover in this chapter about how Elijah remained in position. First, I want you to notice that the drought had lasted three long years. We have certain trials in our lives that last much longer than others. We would like all of them to be short-lived, but that is not always the case. During those times of lengthy trials, we often become weary. We feel that we need to see some sign from God, even a small one that He is working on our situation, and we will soon see breakthrough.

What are we supposed to do during these times? Well, for one thing we should say what we want, not what we have. Like Elijah, we should say, "It is beginning to rain." In other words, whatever blessing we need God to rain into our lives, we speak as if it is already happening. We are not lying when we do this because in the spiritual realm, it is already taking place; we are simply waiting for it to manifest, to come out into the open where we can see it.

During times of need, we should say, "I am blessed. All my needs are met. I have favor everywhere I go. I am blessed when I go in and blessed when I go out. God's blessings are chasing me and overtaking me. I am blessed, blessed, blessed."

When we talk like that, I often wonder how it makes the devil feel. He probably thinks we are confused, that we are not seeing what he is doing, and I am sure that it upsets him that he is not upsetting us.

When we hold fast our confession according to God's Word, there are times when he turns the furnace up seven times hotter, just as he did when Shadrach, Meshach and Abednego refused to bow to the king. They did what the crisis demanded, and then they stood. After the trial was over, they came out of the furnace, and their bodies were not burned — they didn't even smell like smoke. In other words, there was not any trace of evidence that they had even gone through anything. God's deliverance was complete! (Daniel 3.)

Elijah heard something in the spirit. You may not see anything yet, but can you hear anything in the spirit? By faith can you believe your blessing is on the way? The devil may have your blessing dammed up, but the Holy Spirit is pressing against that dam right now, and it is about to burst. Like Elijah, you should be shouting, "You'd better run, Satan, because it's beginning to rain, and my blessings are bursting forth."

ELIJAH KEPT HIS POSITION

So Ahab went up to eat and to drink. And Elijah went up to the top of Carmel; and he bowed himself down upon the earth and put his face between his knees

And said to his servant, Go up now, look toward the sea. And he went up and looked and said, There is nothing. Elijah said, Go again seven times.

1 KINGS 18:42,43

Elijah went up to top of Mount Carmel and took his position.

He bowed down in worship, put his face between his knees and said to his servant, "Go look out toward the sea, and come back and report to me what you see."

The servant went and looked, came back and told Elijah, "There's nothing there." So Elijah said, "Go look again." Seven times that happened, but Elijah never moved out of his position.

What God wants you and me to do is to take our position and, no matter how things may look for a while, maintain that position.

Our problem is that we get into position, but when our situation doesn't seem to change fast enough, we change positions. We start calling everybody we know, asking them what they did when they were in that same situation, or what they would do if they found themselves in that situation. We start reasoning about what we can do to get out of our situation. We must remember that those who trust in the arm of the flesh will be defeated, but those who put their trust in God will never be disappointed or ashamed.

What we must do is take our position and stand. God has said it is going to rain, and it is going to rain. Instead of changing positions, we should look again, and we will see the hand of God moving.

Can't you just see it? Elijah is bowed down while his servant goes to do what he has been told. As he goes to look for rain on the horizon, he is thinking, "Elijah has missed it this time. There is absolutely nothing going on. How long are we going to stay up here and continue this nonsense?"

He comes back and reports to Elijah, and Elijah tells him, **Go again.** Elijah had his mind made up that he was not going to give up. God's Word tells us to set our minds and keep them set. It also warns us against being double-minded, saying that the person who is will never receive anything they ask for from the Lord.

Perhaps the servant said to Elijah, "There's no rain, Elijah. In fact, there are not even any clouds in the sky, and the sun is shining brightly. Elijah, I'm tired of running back and forth, and I don't think it is doing any good. I think that maybe you had better get another word from God. This one doesn't seem to be working."

But Elijah never got out of his position. He continued worshiping God. He didn't even bother getting up and looking at the bleak circumstance. He just said, **Go again.**

When his servant came back with the report each time that there was no rain, Elijah didn't give up just because he heard a negative report. He continued in faith, believing that God was able to bring the rain and knowing in his heart that He would because He had said He would.

ELIJAH OUTLASTED HIS ENEMY

And at the seventh time the servant said, A cloud as small as a man's hand is arising out of the sea. And Elijah said, Go up, say to Ahab, Hitch your chariot and go down, lest the rain stop you.

In a little while, the heavens were black with wind-swept clouds, and there was a great rain. And Ahab went to Jezreel.

The hand of the Lord was on Elijah. He girded up his loins and ran before Ahab to the entrance of Jezreel [nearly twenty miles].

1 KINGS 18:44-46

Finally, the seventh time, Elijah's servant came back and told him that he saw on the far horizon a little cloud about as big as a man's hand.

If you and I could just look at our situation really hard, I am sure we could always find a cloud of hope at least the size of a man's hand. No matter how things may look right now, I am sure that there must be at least that much hope we can hang onto.

The cloud that Elijah's servant saw had to look very tiny in the entire expanse of the sky, but, nonetheless, it was enough to get Elijah excited. Perhaps we should get excited about what we do see, no matter how small it may be, rather than being depressed about what we don't see yet.

As soon as Elijah received the report from his servant, he was bold enough to tell his servant to go and announce to Ahab that he had better head for home because the rain was on its way. Sure enough, in a short time the skies were black with clouds, and a great rain began to fall. Then the Bible says that Elijah girded up his loins and started running so fast that he beat Ahab and his chariot to Jezreel, almost twenty miles away.

Can you just imagine the look on Ahab's face when suddenly Elijah goes running past him, waving and perhaps saying, "I told you so; see you in Jezreel!"

Elijah had outlasted his enemy. He had endured the time of testing, and after it was over, he was still standing in his position. He had worshiped God all the way through the trial, and we must do the same.

When the Spirit of God came on Elijah, he was able to outrun and outlast the enemy, King Ahab. Likewise, when the Spirit of God comes on you and me, we will be able to outrun our enemy, Satan. God's Spirit does come upon us as we worship; He anoints us to outlast the enemy.

Chapter
17

For the Lord Was with Him

And Joseph was brought down to Egypt; and Potiphar, an officer of Pharaoh, the captain and chief executioner of the [royal] guard, an Egyptian, bought him from the Ishmaelites who had brought him down there.

GENESIS 39:1

Do you recall how Joseph came to be in Egypt? It was because, out of jealousy, his own brothers had sold him into slavery to some Ishmaelite traders who had taken him there.

Once he got to Egypt, Joseph was bought by an Egyptian official. But even though Joseph was a slave in the house of Potiphar, God blessed him and prospered him — because He was with him everywhere he went.

Even when we are going through our difficult times, God will bless us *in* them, not just when they are over. The important thing for us to do is keep a good attitude, which includes being thankful for what we do have and giving praise to God, worshiping Him for Who He is.

IN POTIPHAR'S HOUSE

But the Lord was with Joseph, and he [though a slave] was a successful and prosperous man; and he was in the house of his master the Egyptian.

And his master saw that the Lord was with him and that the Lord made all that he did to flourish and succeed in his hand.

That is the way it should be for you. Even if your boss treats you improperly, doesn't see your true value and won't let you do anything but sweep the floor, if God is with you, He can prosper you and make you successful in so many other different ways. God can certainly promote you in His timing because all true promotion comes from the Lord. (Psalm 75:6,7.) Don't look at anything on this earth as your source; look only at God as your Source.

The world will soon recognize that God is with us. Some of those people who have rejected us in the past will see that God is with us; they will see His glory manifest in our lives. If we will just take our position and be faithful in it while we wait on Him, in His timing God will raise us up. It will become obvious and evident to anybody who looks at us that God's hand is upon us for good.

I have seen it happen in my life, and I know many other people who have seen it happen in their lives.

Those people who rejected us and made fun of us, those who said hurtful things to us and about us and did not want anything to do with us because we wouldn't allow them to control us, may end up saying something entirely different.

Actually, I have experienced those who rejected me earlier in life, later trying really hard to become my friend when they saw God's favor on me. I don't want those kind of friends, the kind who are only with us when we are on our way up.

If we will hold our position, having done all the crisis demands, standing firmly in our place of faith, worship and a good confession, we will see that wherever we go, whatever we do, just as God was with Joseph, so He will be with us.

IN PRISON

And Joseph's master took him and put him in the prison, a place where the state prisoners were confined; so he was there in the prison.

But the Lord was with Joseph, and showed him mercy and loving-kindness and gave him favor in the sight of the warden of the prison.

And the warden of the prison committed to Joseph's care all the prisoners who were in the prison; and whatsoever was done there, he was in charge of it.

The prison warden paid no attention to anything that was in [Joseph's] charge, for the Lord was with him and made whatever he did to prosper.

GENESIS 39:20-23

There is really nothing to be worried and upset about if, no matter where you go or what you do, you end up on top, as Joseph did.

I believe that is the way we ought to live: Wherever we go and whatever we do, we ought to see God's goodness and glory manifested in our lives. We should have the best deals, the best positions and the most favor, not because we deserve it as a result of our goodness, but because God is good and wants to express His goodness and favor in the lives of His children. We will go through trials, but they don't last forever and when they are over, we should always be standing firm in our faith.

I believe that the reason that does not happen often enough in our lives is because we have not been taking our position. We have been doing what the Israelites did: despising our situation, grumbling, murmuring, complaining, saying all kinds of negative things, blaming God, blaming other people in our lives, not showing forth the good fruit of the Holy Spirit, being angry, jealous and envious of others whose situations are better than ours.

Only the truth will set us free. We must face truth about where we are in order to get to where we want to be. Facing these kinds of things about ourselves if they apply is not easy, but if we don't face them, we continue deceiving ourselves and remain in bondage forever.

I came to a place in my own life where I had to admit that I just plain had a bad attitude. My problems were not everyone else's fault; they were my fault because I was not doing what God was asking me to do. What He asks of us is not too hard. Through the power of His Spirit, He will enable us to have a good attitude in a difficult situation, if we are willing to do things His way, trusting His timing in our lives.

We should not have a bad attitude and then wonder why we are not being blessed.

There is a better way to live.

18

The Devil Means Evil, but God Means Good

As for you, you thought evil against me, but God meant it for good, to bring about that many people should be kept alive, as they are this day.

GENESIS 50:20

After Joseph had risen to be second in command of all Egypt under Pharaoh, his brothers, who had sold him into slavery, came to Egypt to buy grain during the famine Joseph had predicted would come. Later, Joseph arranged for his father, Jacob, his brothers and all of their families to move to Egypt to live out the rest of the famine in peace and prosperity.

When their father, Jacob, died, Joseph's brothers were afraid that Joseph would try to take vengeance on them for what they had done to him in his youth. Here in this verse we see Joseph's assurance to them of his forgiveness of their wrongdoing toward him. Actually, we see his good attitude being displayed. Notice what he tells them: "You meant it for evil, but God meant it for good, to save many people from starvation."

It is amazing how many times Satan will set a trap for us, meaning it for our harm and destruction. But when God gets involved, He takes that thing that Satan meant to use to destroy us and turns it so that it actually works for our good instead.

Nobody else can make things work out that way, but God can. He can take any negative situation, and through His miracle-working power, use it to make us stronger and more dangerous to the enemy than we would have ever been without it.

My own situation bears this out. I was sexually, mentally and emotionally abused for many years in my childhood. This was certainly a terrible thing to happen to a child and definitely a work of Satan, but God has worked it out for good.

My mess has become my message; my misery has become my ministry, and I am using the experience I gained from my pain to help multitudes of others who are hurting. I encourage you not to waste your pain. God will use it if you give it to Him. He has given me beauty for ashes, just as He promised He would in Isaiah 61:3, but I had to let go of the ashes. I had to learn to have a good attitude, as Joseph did. I had to learn to let go of the bitterness, resentment and unforgiveness I had toward the people who hurt me.

If Satan has already hurt you, don't let the pain go on and on by having a bitter attitude. When we hate people, we are only hurting ourselves more and more. Often the people we are angry at are enjoying their life and are not the least concerned about how we feel about them. Remember, God is your Vindicator, and when the time comes, He will bring justice. In the end the meek inherit the earth, and God's enemies perish. (Psalm 37.)

Let's look at the story of Esther and her people as another example of how God works good out of evil.

SATAN'S PLAN FOR EVIL

And when Haman saw that Mordecai did not bow down or do him reverence, he was very angry.

But he scorned laying hands only on Mordecai. So since they had told him Mordecai's nationality, Haman sought to destroy all the Jews, the people of Mordecai, throughout the whole kingdom of Ahasuerus.

ESTHER 3:5,6

If you are familiar with this story, you remember that Esther, the cousin and adopted daughter of a Jew named Mordecai, had been chosen by King Ahasuerus to be elevated to the position of queen of his kingdom. She was taken into the king's harem as a young maiden, and I feel sure that it was not the plan she had for her life. This situation frightened her, and I am sure that it seemed evil to her at the time. She was there for a period of time, being prepared to go in before the king. When the time came, God gave her favor with him, and she was chosen to be the queen. Little did she know that God was putting her in the position to save a nation.

Often we have a plan in mind for our lives, but something happens to interrupt our plan. We resist and are not happy about the change, but no matter what we do, this new thing seems to be God's will for us. We cannot imagine how it could work out *for* good, but God has a plan in mind that is much better than ours.

In this situation, the Bible tells us that Esther was afraid and did not want to be put in the position she was in. However, Mordecai told her that she was called to the kingdom for such a time as this. In other words, this was her destiny. He also told her that if she did not do what God was asking her to do, she would perish with everyone else. She agreed to do whatever needed to be done.

Mordecai, who was an attendant in the king's court, had an enemy named Haman, the king's highest official. Because Mordecai refused to bow down to him, Haman became angry and hatched a plan to destroy not only Mordecai but also all the Jews along with him — not realizing that Queen Esther was herself a Jew and Mordecai's cousin. (Esther 2:5-23; 3:1-9.)

In the Bible there are some characters who are representatives, or types and shadows, of the enemies of the Lord. One of those is wicked Haman, who represents the devil himself. Haman had a plan for the destruction of God's people, the Jews, just as Satan has a plan for our destruction because we are the people of God.

When Mordecai learned of Haman's evil plan, he told Queen Esther, who invited the king and Haman to an intimate dinner where she hoped to expose Haman's plan to the king.

In Esther 5:11-13 we read what happened when Haman came home to his family and friends after being promoted by the king and given permission and power to destroy all of the Jews in the kingdom.

> And Haman recounted to them the glory of his riches, the abundance of his [ten] sons, all the things in which the king had promoted him, and how he had advanced him above the princes and servants of the king.
>
> Haman added, Yes, and today Queen Esther did not let any man come with the king to the dinner she had prepared but myself; and tomorrow also I am invited by her together with the king.
>
> Yet all this benefits me nothing as long as I see Mordecai the Jew sitting at the king's gate.
>
> ESTHER 5:11-13

Mordecai was a wonderful, godly man who had once saved the king from a plot against him by two of his eunuchs, a deed that had been recorded in the Book of the Chronicles in the king's presence but for which Mordecai had never been rewarded.

Mordecai was a man called and anointed by God to be used to bring deliverance to God's people, just as you and I are called and anointed by God to bring deliverance and help to others in our day.

As we have seen, Haman represents Satan. Just as Haman had a plan for the destruction of Mordecai and the Jews, so Satan has a plan for our destruction.

In Esther 5:14, we see the plan that Haman came up with to destroy Mordecai:

> *Then Zeresh his wife and all his friends said to him, Let a gallows be made, fifty cubits [seventy-five feet] high, and in the morning speak to the king, that Mordecai may be hanged on it; then you go in merrily with the king to the dinner. And the thing pleased Haman, and he caused the gallows to be made.*
>
> ESTHER 5:14

Besides planning the death of Mordecai, with the king's permission, Haman had already issued an order that had been proclaimed throughout the kingdom that on a certain day all the Jews were to be slaughtered and their possessions taken from them.

So Haman had laid a plan for the complete destruction of God's people, one that seemingly could not be changed because it had been issued with the authority of the king's name.

But God had a different plan, and He began to put it into action.

God's Plan for Good

On that night the king could not sleep; and he ordered that the book of memorable deeds, the chronicles, be brought, and they were read before the king.

And it was found written there how Mordecai had told of Bigthana and Teresh, two of the king's attendants who guarded the door, who had sought to lay hands on King Ahasuerus.

And the king said, What honor or distinction has been given Mordecai for this? Then the king's servants who ministered to him said, Nothing has been done for him.

ESTHER 6:1-3

I would like to share a truth with you. Whatever good thing you and I do, even in secret, God has it recorded. He is not going to forget it. The day will come when our good deeds will be brought out into the open.

Every prayer we have prayed, every time we have submitted to authority when we would have liked to rebel against it, every time we have confessed the Word of God when all of our emotions were screaming at us to say negative things — each act of obedience is recorded and will be rewarded. Every time we have taken our position of faith, worship and maintaining a good confession, every time we have offered up to God the sacrifice of praise, God remembers. He does not forget the things we have done right. He has them recorded in His book of memorable deeds, as we read in Hebrews 6:10: **For God is not unrighteous to forget or overlook your labor and the love which you have** shown for His name's sake in ministering to the needs of the saints (His own consecrated people), as you still do.

Mordecai had been doing some good deeds, but he had not been making a big deal out of it. He had just been doing them in secret, unto the Lord. The Word teaches us not to let our right hand know what our left hand is doing where good deeds are concerned. What does that mean? It means to do what we feel God is leading us to do — do it for His glory, then forget it and go on about our business. It means not patting ourselves on the back or telling others what we have done, but simply knowing that our reward will come from God when the time is right.

> The king said, Who is in the court? Now Haman had just come into the outer court of the king's palace to ask the king to hang Mordecai on the gallows he had prepared for him.
>
> ESTHER 6:4

Now we see the scenario coming right down to the wire. We see how the devil, represented here by Haman, is working his plan, and we also see how God is working His plan.

THE TWO PLANS COME INTO CONFLICT

> And the king's servants said to him, Behold, Haman is standing in the court. And the king said, Let him come in.
>
> So Haman came in. And the king said to him, What shall be done to the man whom the king delights to honor? Now Haman said to himself, To whom would the king delight to do honor more than to me?
>
> ESTHER 6:5,6

Because Haman was so full of pride, he couldn't possibly imagine that the king would want to honor anybody other than him. So he thought, "I'm about to really be blessed, so I need to come up with something really good."

And Haman said to the king, For the man whom the king delights to honor,

Let royal apparel be brought which the king has worn and the horse which the king has ridden, and a royal crown be set on his head.

And let the apparel and the horse be delivered to the hand of one of the king's most noble princes. Let him array the man whom the king delights to honor, and conduct him on horseback through the open square of the city, and proclaim before him, Thus shall it be done to the man whom the king delights to honor.

ESTHER 6:7-9

Now watch what happens when Satan's plan and God's plan come into conflict.

Then the king said to Haman, Make haste and take the apparel and the horse, as you have said, and do so to Mordecai the Jew, who sits at the king's gate. Leave out nothing that you have spoken.

ESTHER 6:10

What the king, who represents the Lord in this story, was telling Haman was, "Every blessing you planned for yourself, you are now going to confer on Mordecai. You are going to watch while I bless him." When God decides to bless someone, no person on earth or devil in hell can stop Him.

If God is for us, who can be against us? If God is on our side, what can man do to us?

Oh, I can promise you that Satan has some really nasty tricks in mind for each of us. He has a plan for our total destruction, just as Haman did for Mordecai and the Jews. But God also has a plan for each of us, and God's plan will not be thwarted.

GOD'S PLAN IS NOT THWARTED

Then Haman took the apparel and the horse and conducted Mordecai on horseback through the open square of the city, proclaiming before him, Thus shall it be done to the man whom the king delights to honor.

Then Mordecai came again to the king's gate. But Haman hastened to his house, mourning and having his head covered.

ESTHER 6:11,12

But that is not the end of the story. Not only did the Lord turn the tables on Haman so that he had to give to Mordecai the honor he had planned for himself; He also turned back on Haman the evil plan he had devised for Mordecai.

When Haman went to the dinner that Queen Esther gave for him and the king, she revealed his wicked plot to kill her and her people. As a result, the king had Haman hanged on the same gallows he had built for Mordecai. Esther had worshiped God by her obedience and willingness to stay in a situation that to her was unpleasant. She was willing to lay aside her plan and accept God's plan, even though she did not understand it for a period of time. Each act of obedience is a type of worship that God does not ignore.

Just as Jehoshaphat's enemies and Gideon's enemies ended up being self-slaughtered, so Haman's plan backfired on him. He got what he was trying to give Mordecai and the Jews.

On that day King Ahasuerus gave the house of Haman, the Jews' enemy, to Queen Esther. And Mordecai came before the king, for Esther had told what he was to her.

And the king took off his [signet] ring, which he had taken from Haman, and gave it to Mordecai. And Esther set Mordecai over the house of Haman.

ESTHER 8:1,2

So Mordecai ended up with Haman's house, which had been given to Esther by the king. The king also gave permission and authority to Queen Esther and Mordecai to make a decree and send a letter in his name throughout the kingdom to reverse the orders that Haman had issued to have the Jews killed and their possessions taken from them.

When we keep our eyes on God, stand firm in faith, continue to worship and hold fast a good confession, we will always see the devil's plan for evil in our lives work out for our good and to his demise.

In it the king granted the Jews who were in every city to gather and defend their lives; to destroy, to slay, and to wipe out any armed force that might attack them, their little ones, and women; and to take the enemies' goods for spoil.

The Jews had light [a dawn of new hope] and gladness and joy and honor.

And in every province and in every city, wherever the king's command and his decree came, the Jews had gladness and joy, a feast and a holiday. And many from among the peoples of the land [submitted themselves to Jewish rite and] became Jews, for the fear of the Jews had fallen upon them.

ESTHER 8:11,16,17

When it was all over, the Jews were honored and blessed, Queen Esther was even more admired and respected by the king, and Mordecai had been elevated to second in command under the king himself.

Notice I said, when it was all over. Whatever is going on in your life right now that may be hard for you will eventually be over — *this too shall pass!* I encourage you to look past the pain to the joy of obtaining the prize.

For Mordecai the Jew was next to King Ahasuerus and great among the Jews, and was a favorite with the multitude of his brethren, for he sought the welfare of his people and spoke peace to his whole race.

ESTHER 10:3

As much as I believe anything I have taught, I believe that this is a word in season for our lives, one that we need right now.

Take your position. Don't give up. Stand still. Enter the rest of God. See the salvation of the Lord. Quit worrying and trying to figure out everything that is going on in your life. When temptation comes, take your position and see the salvation of the Lord, which He has planned for you. The battle is not yours; *the battle belongs to the Lord.*

Conclusion

Conclusion

I believe that this is a new day for you and that you will begin to handle your trials in a totally different way as a result of reading this book. You are now in a position to enjoy your life more and to enjoy your walk with God more than ever before. The high calling of each believer is the enjoyment of God. God created us for His pleasure, for fellowship with Him.

If we are worried, we are not fellowshipping. I remember a morning when I sat down in the chair I daily prayed in. I began to worry about whatever my current situation was and to ponder what I was going to do about it. Suddenly, I heard that still, small voice inside of my spirit say, "Joyce, are you going to fellowship with your problem or with Me?" God was willing to handle my problem if I was willing to forget it and spend my time with Him. Remember to worship, not to worry.

Even when you are faced with temptations in your life, you will be strengthened to resist them by worshiping God.

I prophesy to you that you are going to begin to make rapid progress, so much so that you will be amazed. I believe your life will be easier from this point forward. I don't mean that you will never experience trials and testings, but as you worship God, you will find what I call a "holy ease" manifesting in your life. Worshipers find everything to be easier. The burden lifts as we worship, and we are free to enjoy where we are on the way to where we are going.

Oh, worship and magnify the Lord with me — because if God is for us, who can be against us!

Prayer for a Personal
Relationship with the Lord

Prayer for a Personal Relationship with the Lord

God wants you to receive His free gift of salvation. Jesus wants to save you and fill you with the Holy Spirit more than anything. If you have never invited Jesus, the Prince of Peace, to be your Lord and Savior, I invite you to do so now. Pray the following prayer, and if you are really sincere about it, you will experience a new life in Christ.

Father,

> *You loved the world so much, You gave Your only begotten Son to die for our sins so that whoever believes in Him will not perish, but have eternal life.*

> *Your Word says we are saved by grace through faith as a gift from You. There is nothing we can do to earn salvation.*

> *I believe and confess with my mouth that Jesus Christ is Your Son, the Savior of the world. I believe He died on the cross for me and bore all of my sins, paying the price for them. I believe in my heart that You raised Jesus from the dead.*

> *I ask You to forgive my sins. I confess Jesus as my Lord. According to Your Word, I am saved and will spend eternity with You! Thank You, Father. I am so grateful! In Jesus' name, amen.*

See John 3:16; Ephesians 2:8,9; Romans 10:9,10; 1 Corinthians 15:3,4; 1 John 1:9; 4:14-16; 5:1,12,13.

Endnotes

Endnotes

Chapter 3

1. W. E. Vine, *Vine's Complete Expository Dictionary of Old and New Testament Words* (Nashville: Thomas Nelson Inc., 1984), "Nelson's Expository Dictionary of the Old Testament," pp. 184, 185, s.v. "TO PRAISE," "B. Nouns."

2. Vine, "An Expository Dictionary of New Testament Words," p. 479, s.v. "PRAISE," "A. Nouns," "1."

3. Vine, New Testament, p. 479, s.v. "PRAISE," "A. Nouns," "2."

4. Vine, Old Testament, p. 295, s.v. "TO WORSHIP."

5. Vine, New Testament, p. 686, s.v. "WORSHIP (Verb and Noun), WORSHIPING" "A. Verbs," "1."

6. Vine, New Testament, p. 686, "5." *"Notes:"* "(2)" Acts 17:25. See AMP, KJV.

7. Vine, p. 686, "(1)."

8. "In the Garden," words and tune by C. Austin Miles, 1912, copyright © 1912 by Hall-Mack Co. © copyright renewal 1940 (extended), The Rodeheaver Co. All rights reserved. Used by permission of *Baptist Hymnal* © 1975 CONVENTION PRESS, Church and Materials Division, Nashville, Tennessee.

Chapter 11

1. Definition based on Vine, New Testament, p. 639, s.v. "TRANSFIGURE," "TRANSFORM."

Chapter 12

1. MERRIAM-WEBSTER ONLINE:/WWWebster Dictionary. 2002 <http://www.m-w.com> s.v. "behold."

[2] *American Dictionary of the English Language,* 10th Ed. (San Francisco: Foundation for American Christian Education, 1998). Facsimile of Noah Webster's 1828 edition, permission to reprint by G. & C. Merriam Company, copyright 1967 & 1995 (Renewal) by Rosalie J. Slater, s.v. "BEHOLD."

[3] Norvel Hayes, *Worship — Unleashing the Supernatural Power of God in Your Life,* (Tulsa: Harrison House, 1993), pp. 47-53.

Chapter 16
[1] Rick Renner.

ABOUT THE AUTHOR

JOYCE MEYER is one of the world's leading practical Bible teachers. A #1 *New York Times* bestselling author, she has written more than seventy inspirational books, including *The Confident Woman, I Dare You*, the entire Battlefield of the Mind family of books, her first venture into fiction with *The Penny*, and many others. She has also released thousands of audio teachings as well as a complete video library. Joyce's *Enjoying Everyday Life®* radio and television programs are broadcast around the world, and she travels extensively conducting conferences. Joyce and her husband, Dave, are the parents of four grown children and make their home in St. Louis, Missouri.

OTHER BOOKS BY JOYCE MEYER

New Day, New You Devotional

I Dare You

The Penny

The Power of Simple Prayer

The Everyday Life Bible

The Confident Woman

Look Great, Feel Great

*Battlefield of the Mind**

Battlefield of the Mind Devotional

Battlefield of the Mind for Teens

Battlefield of the Mind for Kids

Approval Addiction

Ending Your Day Right

21 Ways to Finding Peace and Happiness

The Secret Power of Speaking God's Word

Seven Things That Steal Your Joy

Starting Your Day Right

Beauty for Ashes (revised edition)

*How to Hear from God**

Knowing God Intimately

The Power of Forgiveness

*Study Guide available for this title.

The Power of Determination

The Power of Being Positive

The Secrets of Spiritual Power

The Battle Belongs to the Lord

The Secrets to Exceptional Living

Eight Ways to Keep the Devil Under Your Feet

Teenagers Are People Too!

Filled with the Spirit

Celebration of Simplicity

The Joy of Believing Prayer

Never Lose Heart

Being the Person God Made You to Be

A Leader in the Making

"Good Morning, This Is God!" (gift book)

Jesus—Name Above All Names

Making Marriage Work
(previously published as *Help Me—I'm Married!*)

Reduce Me to Love

Be Healed in Jesus' Name

How to Succeed at Being Yourself

Weary Warriors, Fainting Saints

Be Anxious for Nothing *

Straight Talk Omnibus

Don't Dread

Managing Your Emotions

Healing the Brokenhearted

Me and My Big Mouth! *

Prepare to Prosper

Do It Afraid!

Expect a Move of God in Your Life . . . Suddenly!

Enjoying Where You Are on the Way to Where You Are Going

A New Way of Living

When, God, When?

Why, God, Why?

The Word, the Name, the Blood

Tell Them I Love Them

Peace

If Not for the Grace of God *

JOYCE MEYER SPANISH TITLES

*Las Siete Cosas Que Te Roban el Gozo
(Seven Things That Steal Your Joy)*

Empezando Tu Dia Bien (Starting Your Day Right)

BOOKS BY DAVE MEYER

Life Lines

TO CONTACT THE AUTHOR,
PLEASE WRITE:

Joyce Meyer Ministries
P.O. Box 655
Fenton, MO 63026
USA
(636) 349-0303
www.joycemeyer.org

Joyce Meyer Ministries—Canada
Lambeth Box 1300
London, ON N6P 1T5
Canada
1-800-727-9673

Joyce Meyer Ministries—Australia
Locked Bag 77
Mansfield Delivery Centre
Queensland 4122
Australia
(07) 3349 1200

Joyce Meyer Ministries—England
P.O. Box 1549
Windsor SL4 1GT
United Kingdom
01753 831102

Joyce Meyer Ministries—South Africa
P.O. Box 5
Cape Town 8000
South Africa
(27) 21-701-1056